Second Chance

Second Chance

Healing Messages
from the Afterlife

Suzane Northrop

JODERÉ
GROUP
San Diego, California

JODERE GROUP, INC.
P.O. Box 910147
San Diego, CA 92191-0147
(800) 569-1002
www.jodere.com

The author of this book does not dispense medical advice
or prescribe the use of any techniques as forms of treatment
for physical or medical problems without the advice of a physician,
either directly or indirectly. The intent of the author is only to offer
information of a general nature to help you in your quest for emotional
and spiritual well-being. In the event you use any of the information in
this book for yourself, which is your constitutional right, the author
and the publisher assume no responsibility for your actions.

Book design by Charles McStravick
Editorial supervision by Chad Edwards

CIP data available from the Library of Congress

ISBN 1-58872-035-7

04 03 02   4 3 2 1
1st printing, May 2002

Manufactured in the United States of America

To Aileen and Max,
the princess and the star

In Memory of
Deanna Davis Davino
and
John Barclay

Contents

Foreword

THERE IS A REASON YOU'VE PICKED UP THIS specific book, and I *believe* it is by *chance*, or *Second Chance* in this case.

Let me explain . . .

Dictionary.com defines chance in the following ways: The unknown and unpredictable element in happenings that seems to have no assignable cause. A *force* assumed to cause events that cannot be foreseen or controlled.

Suzane Northrop lives this definition. Her work and her dedication to her field as a medium has allowed her to help countless thousands in understanding that life and love are eternal by allowing those who have "crossed over"—whom she refers to as the "DPs" or part of the Dead People's Society—to be that *FORCE to cause events that cannot be foreseen or controlled*—to give someone a *SECOND CHANCE* at finding closure and healing . . . and moving forward with their lives after a loss.

Six years ago, Suzane released a groundbreaking book called *The Séance*. In her first work, she introduced herself briefly, discussed the principles of her work, and shared some exercises about understanding the world of energy that we live in.

In the six years since *The Séance* was released, much has happened to its author. Suzane has undergone a metamorphosis both personally and professionally. I can say this, because I watched and experienced it first hand as a friend and colleague.

The Séance was a book that everyone MUST read. And now, *Second Chance: Healing Messages from the Afterlife* revisits that book and **goes beyond.** What Suzane has done, in Suzane Northrop style once again, is clearly groundbreaking.

Realizing the importance of her initial messages brought forth in *The Séance*, she decided to revisit the principles of that innovative work, and has now elected to elaborate more on her contacts and conversations with those on the other side.

Second Chance is autobiographical in nature, yet it's a love story. This book is about death, but I think it is more about life. It speaks of healing and how to deal with relationships in your life today. Some have called it a travel guide, others a how-to manual about connecting with loved ones both here and on the other side. I call it revealing, open, honest, and heartfelt.

For those of you who have read *The Séance,* you will so appreciate the continuing journey and depth in which Suzane now takes you. For those of you who are reading her story for the first time, prepare to open your mind and heart.

What I found most genuine was Suzane sharing with you, the reader, her delving into laboratory conditions to help explain scientifically her abilities. Being a part of the study with her, I was there and watched how difficult it was for her during this time to relive some of her past. Growing up, she knew that she was different from others. This ultimately led her to work with a psychiatrist, and down a road into shock treatment, in an effort to rid her of her "demons." Suzane writes about this for you and shares this personally moving account as she would with a friend. When I asked her why she was being so open and revealing, the answer I received was exactly what I anticipated hearing. She had to. It happened. If she can help someone by sharing her own personal and professional journey, then they might possibly understand his or her own.

Suzane's story and desire to help others began to reveal itself as she and I participated in three phases of ongoing scientific experiments with the Human Energy Systems Laboratory, based out of the University of Arizona, in which we consistently replicated and extended the data to support our work.

Doing this work publicly for over 25 years, she has successfully managed to always put the "work" first, and never "Suzane." Again, I know this firsthand. She had consciously chosen to keep a lower media profile, protecting her "work" as a tiger would protect its cub from the predator known as the media . . . yet managed to build an international reputation that is rock solid, one that is built on her accomplishments, not media commercial hype.

Above and beyond being her friend and colleague, I have also experienced Suzane's abilities on more than one occasion. I have been the recipient of some beautiful messages from my family and friends who are no longer with us in the physical world. So it was a great honor to be asked to write the foreword of this book, to someone who has on more than one occasion, given me . . . a second chance.

— John Edward
Host of TV's *Crossing Over*

Preface

THIS BOOK IS A TRAVEL GUIDE, SOMETIMES A detective story, and a how-to manual. It is a book about death and a book about life.

I am a medium working with those who have crossed over into the *Afterlife*. When I say that, most people laugh, or mumble something polite. I call those with whom I am in contact *DPs*. This is a comfortable term for members of the *Dead People's Society*. If this sounds like I don't take death seriously, nothing could be further from the truth. What is true is that I no longer question what death is or is not; rather, I deal with all the ramifications of the fact that we don't die.

For many, a session with a medium is a second chance. A chance to say, "I'm sorry," "I love you," "Did you suffer?" "I meant to be there," "I always meant to tell you . . .," so that you won't ever again have to say, "If only . . ." For anyone who has suffered a loss, a connection with DPs can be a way of coming to terms with death and resolving lingering conflicts. Whatever it is we cannot forgive or forget or let go, a connection to the DPs can bring healing messages for all our relationships. This holds true for everyone regardless of your belief, skepticism or hidden fear of life after death. It is my hope that what is shared in the pages of this book will help you learn to not be afraid, either for yourself or for those you love who have gone before.

Is there a risk? Yes, the risk of seeing a little more clearly what life is all about. And that is a major risk for some people. Some of us would rather settle for drudgery, boredom, or the dull ache of unresolved issues in relationships that can bring constant sorrow than to rise to that challenge. Finding out more about ourselves and the truth of relationships, past or present, may not be a safe way to go through life. Yet from the DPs' perspective, that's what life was meant to be.

That's the risk. There is no evil here. Communication through a medium to a loved one who has passed is about love, compassion, caring, continuity . . . and quite possibly healing.

> *God did not give us a spirit of timidity,*
> *But a spirit of power, of love,*
> *and of self-discipline.*
>
> — 2 TIM. 1:7

THE DPS GLORY IN THE SPIRIT OF COURAGE IN THE AFTERLIFE. They would like you to find that courage now. That message infuses this book. The corollary to receiving another chance is giving *yourself* another chance, and discovering the courage to face both life *and* death.

Contact with those you love and who have died can enable you to let go of unnecessary grief that may have become a burden or something you cling to resulting in self-recrimination. Through these contacts, you will find opportunities that provide resolution to pain and relationship problems once thought to be beyond all hope of solving. The ultimate discovery is peace of mind.

Second Chance: Healing Messages from the Afterlife is written for anyone who is afraid of or uncertain about death. If you can come to believe that death is not the end, you will release unlimited potential within yourself. You will also have conquered your greatest fear. This book is also for those who have themselves had contact with the *spirit world*—whether this terrified them, confused them, or exhilarated them. Whether they have told anyone or kept it quietly to themselves. Now you can know, indisputably, that your experiences are real and valid. It is my desire that the sharing of experiences and learning techniques in these pages will help you to understand that you do not walk alone.

I know there are skeptics.

It is not my job or my place to convince you of what I believe—that we do not die. You don't even have to believe in mediums. You need only have an inquiring mind, open to the possibilities of life. I never intended to become a medium, but here I am. I am now quite certain that mine is a tough, demanding job with perhaps the ultimate in *work-place stress*. I have spent a lot of time defending my job.

Since we first found out about fallibility, humanity has been struggling with the concept of death. Respect is due to all who have been truly seeking an honest answer, no matter what the state of sophistication of their methodology, their prose, or their belief systems. There is now a growing body of research in my field, and wonderful people, practitioners, researchers, and philosophers.

Recent discoveries in physics regarding energy and matter have given new credibility to psychic phenomena, to mediumship, and to works of other ages and other belief constructs concerning life's continuing passages. It is also true that there have been exposes, cold-hearted scams, gullible people, tear-jerking stories in the tabloids, and sensationalism. This is why, I suppose, I can't be *chin-out* determined to convince you.

Convince me of what? you ask.

Convince you of what you're not sure you really want to hear and might even refuse to consider if you did hear it.

For the record, I come to you with these beliefs:

▲ There is a *Higher Power*.

▲ Life is a series of relationships.

▲ Death is a continuation of many of those relationships.

▲ Relationship problems should be worked out here, because they don't go away—and it is a lot harder working them out later.

▲ Many of us don't work out the problems for so many different reasons, and are left with grief, guilt, or anger when the other person passes on.

▲ You are able to work out your problems with the dead even after they have passed on.

▲ You'll receive information from the DPs, but not instructions. Guidance: yes; decisions: no. They will not interfere with your path.

And finally, I wish to say that I believe I have been given a gift and the *Higher Power* intends that I share it with others.

There is a continuum of life and a continuum of relationships. I help the DPs, the speakers in *Spirit,* contact the living to work on relationships (which the DPs also have trouble letting go of) so that you and they can get on with the rest of your lives.

— Suzane Northrop

Life is eternal and love immortal
and death is only a horizon,
and a horizon is only the
limit of our sight.

— Anonymous

Acknowledgments

I RESPECTIVELY THANK ALL WHO HAVE GIVEN me the privilege and honor to connect with their loved ones who have crossed over, and who have so generously shared their personal stories.

During my travels, I have had the good fortune to meet many radio and TV personalities. I would especially like to thank Gary Craig of WTIC, Hartford, Connecticut, for "getting my work," and sharing it with such passion to his listeners. In addition, Art Sears for being one of the best producers in the business. He treats his guests with the utmost respect.

A heartfelt thanks to John Edward for his friendship, and caring for the work as I do.

This book could not have happened without the vision and tenacity of Debbie Luican. The Jodere Group is a clear reflection of her commitment to help change the world.

My appreciation to Chad Edwards for his brilliant editing, allowing my voice to always be heard.

A special thanks to Linda Manning, my assistant, for her amazing patience and caring for clients, and keeping my life in order.

Finally, my humble gratitude to the *DPs,* who have allowed me to share *my* gift and *their* message to the world so all may know that **love *is* eternal.**

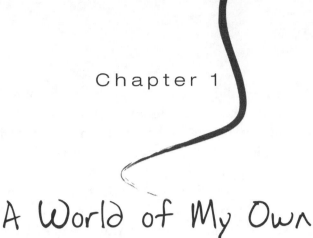

Chapter 1

A World of My Own

WHEN I WAS FIVE, AN EVENT SEEMED TO accelerate my connection with the *Spirits*. It was a gorgeous day about to be made better with ice cream. I hated holding adults' hands, and as I looked longingly at the ice cream parlor across the street, I couldn't wait for the treat anymore. I yanked my hand away from my mother and ran into the street. Suddenly, without notice, I was hit by a car and thrown into the air.

My shoes and socks flew one way and I flew another, landing with a dull thud on the street. I remember my mother crying all the way to the hospital, and someone saying that if it hadn't been a Buick bumper the kid would have been a *goner*. To this day, my mother still drives a Buick.

The accident did not cause major injury, but it allowed a door that seems stuck in most humans to become unstuck, and then swing wide open. It's my theory that the mild concussion kick-started, whether I wanted it or not, my ability as a psychic and medium.

Several months after my accident, I woke up one night and saw a man standing in my bedroom. I wasn't frightened, rather the contrary. I was fascinated because I had never seen anyone in my hometown like him. He looked like Charlie Chan of the movies, including the mustache.

I can't really explain what he said, because I didn't hear words. I experienced a feeling that he was there, somehow, to protect and take care of me. This is very hard to describe. It was so real, yet so abstract. I comprehended it, and yet I didn't.

In any case, I was wildly excited. I wanted to share my friend. I got out of bed and ran downstairs to tell my father about the wonderful man in my room. He grabbed his shotgun and took the stairs two at a time, stubbing his toe on the way leaving a stream of blood and curses. By the time he and I got there *Charlie* was gone. I was very upset. I felt my father had chased him away.

These escapades continued for three nights. I went through the same ritual each night with my father coming up the stairs with the shotgun, a little more slowly and resignedly each time. My parents didn't share my enthusiasm, and by the third night they didn't even believe me. Just to be sure, they made me sleep with the light on. To this day, I cannot sleep comfortably in a lighted room.

FROM THIS INITIAL CONTACT WITH THE SPIRIT WORLD, I learned several lessons, although I didn't always heed them. First was that others were unaware of the presences that were so real to me, and even more important for me later, that they were threatened by them.

My paternal grandmother was a very influential presence in my life. She was a tough woman, leaving my irascible grandfather at a time when a rural woman just didn't do such things. She had three sons. The oldest stayed on the farm with my grandfather, the second one died of tuberculosis, and the third, my father, went with her. My grandmother took on many odd jobs, but the steadiest was housekeeping for a farmer. It was while working on that farm that my grandmother had a very bad car accident. She recovered and also received a sizable insurance settlement. Nothing is coincidence. This happened during the Depression and the farmer was about to lose his farm. My grandmother offered to buy the farm and have the farmer continue to work it. He agreed. She liked the idea of this so much she turned it into a business. She traveled the county, knocking on doors at other farms, telling farmers that if they wanted to sell, she would find a buyer. Later, she bought and sold residential houses as well. My grandmother became the most successful real estate broker in Chemung County, in western New York state.

MY FATHER, WHO WAS LIVING WITH HER, REMAINED HER favorite, which had its downside. She loved him, but the shadow she cast overwhelmed a basically insecure man. He remained forever a bit of a mommy's boy. He eventually joined her real estate business, although he hated it.

When I was born, my father really didn't want me. So, he kept the birth a secret from my grandmother, and ordered his new young wife, my mother, to have me adopted. I learned this story, years later, in a cozy conversation with my maternal grandmother. We had been talking about houses, and I was recalling the apartment I remembered as a child. She told me that I didn't live in an apartment. I lived in a house. "But I *do* remember the apartment," I insisted. Then she said that what I was remembering was when I was living with the hospital social worker. A silence suddenly fell over the room and the color left her face. She realized what she had said. It was the secret I was never supposed to know.

It seems the social worker apparently couldn't bear to see me given up for adoption. Out of her love for this child, she took me from the hospital to her apartment until eventually my parents were convinced to take me back. I think she might have kept me herself in the case my parents hadn't decided to reverse their decision of adoption. I never met this kind woman, and never knew her name.

I do know that for years, I would ride my bicycle by a slightly shabby apartment building and feel curiously drawn to it. But I never knew why, never looked to see who might live there, just pedaled home.

My father covered this up and presented me, at six months, to his mother with some explanation of my being sickly and in the hospital. He explained his way out of it by telling her they didn't want to worry her. So, here was her favorite son's first child, and my grandmother was overjoyed. And family life went on.

My paternal grandmother moved among the business elite of the county, and wanted very much to have a musician in the family. She liked music well enough, but she also wanted to be able to casually drop into the conversations something like, "Oh, he's the musician in the family." My dad was her choice for the role. He was very talented, but lacked the discipline for the demanding study and practice of music, something he was bluntly honest about. So, the first-born grandchild, me, was plunked down on a piano bench. I started playing at the age of four, and soon after, my grandmother bought me a brand new piano.

Music became my passion. I can't remember when I didn't love it. Before I learned to play, I would find peace in listening. As I look at it now, my passion for music was not only because of my love for the rich sounds, but because music took me "elsewhere" as my family surroundings grew more and more unhappy. "Elsewhere" was a beautiful world of sound and melody which, somehow, gradually opened into the *Spirit World* as well. I had no need of the fantasy world so many lonely children create. I had music and the *Spirits*. One I could talk about and the other I couldn't.

I remained the only child, and my grandmother's favorite until the age of nine. Raised in a small rural town, I spent most of my time playing alone or engaged in my music. My mother would remark to her friends that I came home from school each day wondering why I didn't have a brother or sister. My persistent hints worked: My mother went for a medical check-up. Had something been wrong? I don't know, but I would soon have two sisters within four years. I was very happy when my first sister was born. I couldn't wait for her to grow up so I could have someone to play with. I didn't know that wasn't going to happen. She would grow up and I would soon have another younger sister, but neither ever became my playmate. Instead, I became their caretaker.

I know a lot about the *caretaking* instinct. I have seen it work for good and for bad in my clients. I know a lot about the sense of abandonment also, physical and emotional. My father and mother didn't much like each other, and didn't want to stay home and play "family." Each went out almost every evening; my father without a word, and my mother with a "Suzane, look after the kids."

When I was 13, the year my second sister was born, my paternal grandmother was diagnosed with cancer of the colon. My father became emotionally paralyzed and unable to talk about the situation. He blamed everyone else for the illness; a kind of crazed lashing out that I've seen over and over again in my practice. He felt threatened while she was ill and abandoned when she died. My mother didn't dare speak about it either, and I was to be quiet and take care of my sisters. Heaviness permeated the house. My sisters and I tried to be seen and not heard, but we had no idea what was happening.

This sense of abandonment is a constant theme in my work now, as is the need for people to redirect their anger and pain. What I saw as a child in my father and mother, I see again every day and sometimes I think I need to wear an emotional bulletproof vest. And, virtual earplugs.

An example is when a woman came to me recently, telling me she had tried to see another medium, but he wouldn't see her. So, I was it! Not by choice, but by default.

The session began and immediately her mother came through. The woman tensed; it was apparent this was the person she had hoped to contact. Her mother's information was clear as a bell; her name, manner of death, who was over there with her. Suddenly the woman began yelling at her, and yelling at me, since I was in the middle. She spent 45 minutes ranting and raving at her mother's spirit. "If you hadn't smoked, you wouldn't have died, Mom. But you did smoke, and so you died, and left me alone and you've made my life a mess!" Her phrasing was a little rougher, but you get the point. She finally left, rehashing her anger at the other medium, who wouldn't see her.

That was one of the nights I went to bed early.

There have been so many other instances over the years. Some people I can help, and some I cannot. I couldn't help my father. I was too little and he didn't want it anyway. He found his consolation in a bottle. I couldn't help my mother. She left her mess of a family and went out every night with her friends. I *could* help my sisters by watching over them, and I could help myself. I could also, later on, help others I would find out. A medium is able to bring reconciliation and peace, if allowed.

As a child, of course, I could not foretell any of this. The earlier years had been lonely, and now at 13, I was faced with the fact that the person who loved me most was dying with colon cancer.

I was not allowed to see my grandmother very much after she went into the hospital. On my last visit, I could see she was not the grandmother I had known. She had been a robust woman, 170 pounds of drive and perseverance. This was a woman ahead of her time. One, who had started a successful business from scratch. Now she just seemed to be dwindling away. I couldn't comprehend.

A week after that hospital visit, early in the morning, my grandmother came into my bedroom and woke me up. I was ecstatic! Grandma was herself again, big, fat, and most important, out of pain. Half asleep, I stood hugging her, feeling that with her well again my father and my family would be back to *normal*. She told me she wanted me to continue with my piano lessons and that she was going to give me her ruby ring with the diamond in it. She couldn't visit me often, she said, but if I needed her, I could think of her and she would always be in my thoughts and my heart. I was so happy to see her again I really didn't pay much attention to what she was saying. I didn't mention the visit because I assumed everyone already knew Grandma had gotten well again.

The following morning my mother came into my bedroom looking harried and informed me I would have to take care of my younger sisters, as there were things she and my father needed to attend to in regard to Grandma. I thought this odd, but in my family it was safer not to ask questions. The next day my mother told me I was to get dressed up because we were going to the parlor to see Grandma. My father was already there, waiting for us. I wasn't quite sure what a parlor was, but I figured there was going to be a party in honor of Grandma's recovery. My sisters were too young to go, my mother said.

Mother didn't say a word during the car ride. I could tell she'd been crying. I didn't understand why because I thought we are going to the parlor to celebrate Grandma's getting well. Parents sure are strange. Still, I didn't dare ask questions. We drove into the driveway of a large house. There was a fairly big parking lot on the left filled with cars. No doubt belonging to all the people attending the party. An attendant opened the door for my mother and me, and he solemnly told us to go in.

We entered a large room filled with flowers and chairs lined up in rows, similar to a recital or concert. People were standing in small groups whispering. I walked around exploring the room, wondering what would happen next. I walked past a box in the front. There lay a woman made up and dressed to look like my grandmother. She was even wearing my grandmother's best dress. Why would someone dress up a dummy in my grandmother's clothes and put her in a box for everyone to stare at, I thought?

Suddenly, I became aware my grandmother was standing next to me. There she was, looking great and doing fine. I must have started talking to her and had been seen because my mother ran up to me, very annoyed, and scolded me for upsetting my father. "What are you doing? You are being completely disrespectful! Go to the car and wait for us." So, Grandma and I went and sat in the car.

After an hour or so, my parents came to the car. My father took off speeding through our town's one street, my grandmother sitting next to me, clearly disapproving of my father's driving. Since I was already in trouble for talking to Grandma, I didn't tell my father that she was sitting next to me and how upset she was with him for going so fast.

Maybe you think I must have been pretty dumb for not realizing that my grandmother had died. But to me, she looked more beautiful and relaxed after what people termed "death" than she did when she was in pain and had lost so much weight. And I knew what I knew, even after hearing people say she had died. I could still *see* Grandma vividly. I don't mean I was less upset, or that the loss didn't affect me, but somehow I felt safe. I knew she was someplace else, but close. And I knew she would visit me, and me alone. That, I kept to myself.

That was the beginning of my conversations with the Dead People's Society. Grandma kept her promise: she still visits me, not all the time, but when she's got something to say.

GROWING UP, I KNEW I WAS "DIFFERENT," THE WORST calamity that can befall a teenager. Part of this, I thought, was because of the turmoil in our family, and the fact that I almost never could accept invitations to go anywhere. As I said before, I had to stay home to take care of my sisters while my parents went out. So, gradually, I stopped getting invitations.

Meanwhile, things would happen that I knew about in advance. There were little things: knowing who it was when the phone rang or who was going to have a baby. I told myself at the time, why did I have to know something that I could not help and could do nothing to prevent? I hated that. I also hated being stared at, which was becoming more and more common, because I talked to myself a lot. At least that's what it looked like to my neighbors and the kids at school. They didn't know about the DPs, or my sense of another world. And, I wasn't telling. I compensated for my many levels of being different by becoming one of the wildest kids in town. The upside was that I always knew someone was protecting me. One instance can still shake me, and still cause me to offer a prayer of thanks.

My father kept guns in the house. Our family knew it; most of the neighbors and neighbors' kids knew it. My mother hated the gun collection, because long ago her brother had been killed by a ricocheting rifle bullet. I was wary of guns, but also saw them as "cool" and a powerful symbol.

One of the neighborhood boys, Gary, came to visit one afternoon. I told him I was not in the mood and wanted him to leave. He just stood there. I told him again to leave, adding that if he didn't he'd be sorry. He wasn't being aggressive, just stubborn, but I decided to teach him a lesson.

I went to my parents' bedroom and reached for my father's .22 pistol. His guns were always kept unloaded, and I didn't look for the cache of bullets; I just wanted to play a power game. I walked back into the kitchen where Gary was still ostentatiously lounging. I pointed the gun at Gary's head and pulled the trigger four or five times, pretending to be angry. Then I felt one of the most intense psychic jolts I have ever experienced. I was pulling the trigger again when something yanked my hand up vertically toward the ceiling. *The gun went off.*

I broke down in terror, while Gary ran out the door. Even now when I think about this, my blood curdles. Later, we discovered it was the boy next door who had put the single bullet in my father's gun as a joke. No one will ever convince me that God did not intervene. I have never since picked up a gun, and I never will.

Life in my home had never been *normal* before my grandmother's death. But when she died all hell broke lose. My father continued to fall apart. He went on rampages, smashing all my grandmother's pictures. A man, who earlier, never took a drink was now drinking a quart of whiskey a day. We hid from his anger and his guns. I hid, quite literally, and spiritually, reaching to the *other world* more and more for safety.

And then there were uglier things. The premonitions I tried to deny myself. Like with my friend, Paul. I didn't want to know that he was going to lose his leg on the railroad tracks. I was so upset that day, I didn't dare go near the tracks, but I told myself I didn't know anything. It was a Tuesday afternoon. I remember, because there were tryouts for the school play, *Annie Get Your Gun*. I desperately wanted to be in it, but knew it was hopeless. Anything that required nighttime activities was out. I had kids to watch, my sisters. So I left school and began walking home, feeling very sorry for myself.

Then, suddenly, I felt a sick, sinking feeling in my stomach. Something terrible had happened. I ran into our house, and asked my mother, *What happened?* She replied, *Nothing has happened.* I then ran next door to our neighbor. Again I was told that nothing had happened, as she looked at me appraisingly. As I was leaving her house I saw Alan, Paul's brother, running up the road, shrieking hysterically, "Paul. It's Paul!" After that, it seemed that crowds of people and ambulances were everywhere.

One of the favorite young male games on testosterone-pumping spring afternoons was to stand at the side of the railroad tracks, and as the train slowed, jump onto an open freight car. Paul had stood with the other boys, poised, waiting, as the train clackety-clacked slower. Then, he jumped, but he stumbled. His pants caught on a rail, and his leg went under the steel wheel of the train. His leg was completely severed.

Since those early days, many people have told me that a religious upbringing could have provided me comfort and stability. That my father could have also found comfort in religion. Maybe, but none of my family is or was religious in any formal churchgoing sense. There were no restrictions in my family from religious dogma. My mother had a solid belief in God as a strong, spiritual power, but she had no set religion to accompany that. I didn't notice the lack as a child except that it was just one more thing we didn't do as a family. Actually, I was the only one in my family who attended church. Not for the sermons, but for the music. That was the way God talked to me. I believe traditional religions have a part in our lives, but it's also true that Western religions frown on attempting to make contact with the dead. Besides, I already felt different enough in those days. So, I kept quiet about talking to dead folks. People used to get burned alive for that.

I have to say that my lack of religious upbringing has sometimes left me stranded. I believe in God, a *Higher Spirit*, but not the standard orthodox version. People trying to belittle what I do frequently throw various tracts and dogmas at me. I don't agree with them in any case, but I don't always recognize the *proof* they're going on and on about. If any of my family had been formally religious, and I had absorbed some of it, it might have helped me with some of my clients. I mean that honestly, and conscientiously, because I try very hard to empathize with religious feelings people bring to sessions with the DPs. I have studied various religions in some degree, to understand my clients better and to broaden my knowledge of the *Spirit World*.

As my Grandma had requested, I had no problem with continuing my music lessons. After all, music was my life. In my late teens, I was desperate to play in a rock and roll band. I asked my father if there were some way he could help me financially, so that I could get a keyboard, amplifiers, and the other equipment to play in a band. A forlorn hope, I thought, since musical instrument equipment is very expensive, and my father was tight with his wallet. He stunned me by agreeing, and took me off on a happy buying spree in music stores. Up until that moment, we had spent so little quality time together that our dad/daughter shopping trip became an icon to me of what a relationship with my father might have been like. I have since concluded that he had come to the end of his intense craziness phase and was beginning to mellow. I didn't know that at the time; I just thought I had lucked out and found him on a good day. This was only one of a few bright spots I experienced with my father. For the most part, he was horrible to live with through those long years of growing up.

Before long a band was born.

My band was good. We played local colleges and anywhere else we could get bookings. During this time I met a woman from New York City who was a student at Syracuse University. We both shared a great love of music, and a wonderful friendship followed. Then she had decided to return to New York City. This raised several issues for me. The other band members and I were having serious conflicts of personality and ambition. I wanted out, even more than they wanted me out. I had 30 dollars in my pocket. And I hated my home life. I decided this was a message.

Chapter 2

Nobody Wants to Be a Medium When They Grow Up

So, AT 19, I PACKED MY BAGS, TOOK MY thirty dollars, got into my Nash Rambler ("Faithful George"), and headed for New York City. I decided that knowing one person there was enough, and that it was a toss-up, which would be more destructive to me, living in the *Big City*, or staying at home. Little did I know, God had other ideas in store for me besides music; moving to New York City would be the beginning. It wasn't until I moved there that I realized how easily I connected to the other world and that most people didn't.

When I arrived, I discovered my friend lived in Westchester with her family, and they had no room for me. I was on my own.

I knew that even if one moves to New York to set the world on fire, the first priority is a real job to pay the rent. I decided that if I couldn't write music right away, at least I would be around it. I got a job at the biggest music store in New York. That was the last real job I ever had. It didn't take me long to learn that people viewed me as different. I couldn't figure out whether it was because I was a rural, small-town girl or an eccentric artist. The other salespeople at the store considered me very strange. Could it have been that I advised people on music selections, and that sometimes it slipped out what their DPs would be saying?

It was a confusing time. While everyone was looking at me as if I were strange, I was living in a hotel in the arm pit of New York , and for the first time in my life, I met prostitutes, drag queens, and druggies. You name it. It was all too close to the scene from the movie, *Big*, where the Tom Hanks's character whimpers on the bed in the sleazy hotel as gunshots whiz by outside his door. Thank God, Bobby, a friend I had met while working at the music store, lived there too. He was the only person I was close to. My father never talked to me now, and my mother didn't call me because she was angry at the loss of her babysitter.

Mostly, I was very alone. Childhood revisited. Shades of my traumatic teens. I was mumbling to the DPs, but again, I didn't know it. I didn't see them. I felt a presence. I didn't know who or what it was, but it was always there; shimmering just on the edge of my consciousness. Most people daydream, fall into reveries, talk to themselves. There are many half-lives of the mind and many levels of being between waking and dreaming. My equivalent was a conversation with that presence; most often internally, yet sometimes verbal. I was always mentally composing music as well, so tunes and chords would fill my mind as often as the daily news or the routines of my life, and always with that presence quietly, supportively in the background. While this was richly satisfying, it didn't make me a social success. I did seem to handle it better than I had in my teens, because I could always come home to Bobby.

I walked the streets alone, a lot. There is no question God and the DPs had something for me to do because I could so easily have been killed.

One day at work I saw a man walk into the store. Nothing unusual about that, but, immediately, the DPs gave me a message: he was planning to steal as many records as he could. I did the right thing by informing the manager of the man's intentions.

"Do you see the guy wearing a black hat and plaid pants and carrying a tan overcoat? He's trying to fill up his brief case with as many records he can walk off with."

The manager then asked me, "How do you know?" I proudly replied, "The DPs are telling me." He looked at me strangely.

I was well aware one has to be tactful in potential theft encounters, so to make sure, I once again tuned into the DPs to double check my information. A moment later, I would say, "Yes, I'm positive, he's a thief" The manager just stood there, shaking his head and walked away. He said nothing and didn't even try to follow the man. I was very upset and highly insulted. Here I had given him valuable information and he wasn't acting on it. I don't think I had yet fully realized that however normal it was for me to talk to the other world, it wasn't so normal for others, and perhaps I should not be so free in sharing my knowledge with other people. The frustrating part was that while the manager was trying to figure out if I was losing it, the guy in the ugly plaid pants sauntered out with at least 20 records in his briefcase.

Of course word moved like wildfire around the store that I had gone off the deep end, hearing voices from the *other world*. A cashier suggested I needed help and should go to Bellevue. I didn't even know that was a hospital specializing in psychiatric cases.

Bobby had a small circle of friends, and a best-buddy-until-we-die relationship with a friend since childhood, Peter. Peter was also living in our miserable hotel until he could find his own place together with his girlfriend.

Bobby's friends accepted me, and I leaned on them as well as on Bobby. I'm not sure how much of our closeness was due to my intense loneliness as a hick in the *Big City*, or worse, a hick who talked to herself, or so people thought.

Then Peter committed suicide. His romance, the big one, the real one he was so sure of, had shattered. He took the window way out, seven floors down to concrete. Bobby was devastated. We had to leave the hotel, he said. We had to get out. Things hadn't been going well for me at work, so I followed Bobby to a new apartment, thinking we would have a better life and a better existence. It didn't happen that way.

Bobby never was the same. He blamed himself about Peter's suicide, positive that he should have intuited something was wrong and that a "real friend" could have found out and helped. He tried to cope, but something deep inside him, some internal strength, had broken. He got involved with the wrong people. When some of them started coming to our door, I knew it was time for us to move out of the city altogether. Bobby agreed and it was decided that New York wasn't for us anymore. San Francisco became the new destination. A week later, we were on our way. I was sure it was going to be the start of a new life.

Within two months of our arrival in San Francisco we decided to go our separate ways. I got the stereo, records and the car. After leaving, I deliberately stayed out of touch with Bobby. I didn't want to know what he was going to do, since I already knew somewhere inside myself. That wasn't premonition or the DPs: it was the simple recognition of another human being bent on self-destruction. Some months after I left, Bobby overdosed and died.

I couldn't have helped Peter and I couldn't help Bobby either. I didn't blame myself for either death, but I was conscious I hadn't been able to help.

San Francisco was the beginning of my own gold rush. The dead folks were pounding down the door. Their presence in my life was becoming more and more pronounced. I seemed to have little control around when and where they would show up. I mean, I was completely being bombarded by the *spirit folks* and was having difficulties adjusting. From what I could figure, they were trying to let me know they were around and this was beginning to create some problems. The minute I would meet someone, friend, foe, or possible date, *their* dead relatives would show up. Not great for relationships! Who needs to know all these things, especially when first meeting someone and there are all his dead relatives!

In New York, I had met a woman, Joyce, a native San Franciscan. She had moved to New York to try to find success in the theater. She finally threw in the towel and returned home. Stranded with no place to go and very little money after Bobby and I parted ways, I called her. She graciously invited me to her parent's home to stay.

Joyce's mother was a psychiatrist, and I thought maybe she could lead me in the right direction in understanding the presence of the DPs. I needed some guidance, some answers. So I opened up and began to share what was going on. Bad move.

She didn't mean any harm, but in her professional opinion people who speak to empty spaces are probably psychotic. This was the '70s, and even in a city exploding with expression like San Francisco's Haight Ashbury, people who talk to what no one else *saw* were thought of as "nuts" or schizophrenic. She recommended me to a colleague of hers. After one visit, he suggested I take drugs or consider shock treatment. He didn't think I was any danger to others, just myself, so he decided that shock treatment on an out-patient basis was the quickest avenue for results. (I think now possibly he just wanted to be "done" with me, and felt an obligation to his colleague, Joyce's mother.) So I decided to "go with the flow" and trust these people. *Wrong.* I can't begin to tell you the horrific experience that was. And, it did little to quell the DPs. In fact, they felt the need to protect me and make their presence known even more. After six months of this, I was declared incompetent and placed on disability.

Finally, I found the strength within myself to say, "Enough!" One thing I had always known was that I wasn't crazy. So, in little more than six months from my arrival, I once again packed myself up and headed deeper into northern California. I decided I would look for a place in the hills where I could work as a live-in caretaker, and basically be left alone. I ultimately found a house with no water or electricity, but with room for my piano. Here, I would teach piano, compose music, and figure out my fate. There had to be a reason why I had the uncanny ability to "tap in" to another world; the dimension where the dead folks lived. Once I understood this, I could rejoin the human race.

ON A SIDE NOTE HERE, YEARS LATER I WOULD BE CONTACTED by HBO to participate in a special documentary they were doing called *Life After Life*. I would be working with other known mediums: John Edward, Reverend Anne Gehman, Laurie Campbell, and George Anderson. It happened that John and I had known each other since he was about 17. We reconnected when I contacted him to ask what his thoughts were around doing this.

In addition to all this, the people associated with the documentary came and filmed me during a seminar, and also attended a radio show I was doing. As it came to be, the only part of the special they wanted me for was the testing segment. With this information, and after a conversation with John, I was pretty sure I didn't want to be a part of this. So, I graciously declined and walked away. I could see that the scientists were trying to do their study with honor, yet it seemed to have little to do with mediumship.

They kept calling back, and I actually turned down the pursuit to be involved three times. They were unwavering and insistent that I was important to this project because I had been doing my work for 25 years. They were committed to the fact that memory and information was never lost, only evolving. They had already been posing questions about systemic memory like "Does the heart remember?" "Does water remember?" "Does the soul remember?" and were now ready to lay the groundwork for future research that could potentially prove whether consciousness survives physical death. This is why we became an important component to the study. They had already documented startling cases of organ transplant patients who had experienced cellular memories of their donors, and wanted to take it a step further.

Finally, I agreed to do it. John was "on board" so that felt a bit more comfortable. I had also pursued a lengthy discussion with one of the scientists and director that helped my decision about going forward with the project. I realized I had been suggesting to clients and seminar attendees for quite some time to listen and trust their own messages from beyond. Here, I had the opportunity with a respected scientist, Gary E.R. Schwartz, Ph.D., to contribute to a deeper understanding and validation of life after death and continued consciousness. Dr. Schwartz had been wading through quite a bit of flack regarding his research, yet was determined to see it through. I thought if he was willing to put his reputation on the "line" to eliminate any shred of doubt, so could I. It was important for me also to have people understand that these communications were authentic, so here was my chance to have that documented and validated on record. My decision was also based on additional facts that this project was being backed by a well-respected company, HBO, and one of the producers was Linda Ellerbee, whom *I* respected.

We were flown to Tuscon for the filming. The day before we were briefed about what was to come. John nominated me to be the *first up* for the day, and I once again went with the flow. It was also revealed during the briefing that it had been decided, at the last minute, we would be "wired up" just to add to the validity of the study. Of course, in my mind I am thinking like an EKG or EGG. "OK," I thought, "I can do that."

The next morning I arrived to find that the wires were to be attached to my head for the taping! Silently, my heart sank to the floor; shades of the past shock treatment of the '70s ran through my mind in *recall*. For a split second, I thought of turning and running out. Yet, I gathered myself, took a breath, and agreed to let them put the wires on my head as it came time for me to "do my thing." We were then led to a separate part of the lab so we would have no contact with the "sitters" (the people we were reading) until they were ready.

Interestingly enough, some well-known skeptics had been invited to view the video tapings at one point, as was a leading magician. The magician was asked to study the tapes to see if he could detect any "trickery" being used to get information. His feedback was that only if I had hired private investigators or had known the person(s) prior (which I had not), could I have delivered the information to the participants I did. The skeptics, when invited to see additional tapes from the follow-up sessions, interestingly enough declined.

After the HBO taping, I personally spoke to Dr. Schwartz and explained the past "shock stuff." He was taken aback and went on to say how honored he was that I would go through this considering what had happened to me before. For me, it all had presented an opportunity to conquer the past and make history in the same process. What is it they say, "To move on, we need to fight the demons and fears?"

We were to go back two other times to continue the process after the production. Gary was adamant about having the best conditions scientifically so he could put the results on record. The testing went very well and an account is being included in the new book he has co-authored with William L. Simon called *The Afterlife Experiments: Breakthrough Scientific Evidence of Life After Death*, due out in Spring 2002. The team scored an 80 percent accuracy as a group on the testing of the HBO documentary. Dr. Schwartz later stated that the thrill of the high accuracy percentages, and the quality of the material that was so often penetratingly accurate, was only marred by the poor editing done by HBO in the end for their entertainment advantage.

AFTER FOUR YEARS OF SECLUDED LIFE AND COMPOSING A WEALTH of music, I knew it was time to move again. Somehow it was made clear that I should move to the *City of Angels*. I'd never been there. California has always been considered the center for involvement in metaphysics, and Los Angeles is the capital. The dogs I had acquired and I packed up; we arrived there a month later.

The DPs said I needed to go to college and get my degree in music. So I did, attending California State University of Los Angeles. It was only fitting that I expand my horizons musically. It was, however, not the only horizon

I would expand. It was here that I would meet other people, psychics, delving into other realms. This was very exciting to actually meet others who shared some of my gifts and my conflicts. I was in my mid-twenties, so a lot of things were exciting.

It was during this time that I met Helen. After a few random get-togethers, she invited me to her home. It was the first time I felt I could sit and talk to someone who understood my plight. Within minutes she said to me, "We need to talk about your open line to the *other world*." Helen was a medium herself and this was the first time I heard the word mediumship, and what it meant, the good and bad parts. I talked to Helen mostly about confusion and about being ridiculed. Then she told me her story.

An only child, she was born and raised in Oklahoma where her father was a Baptist minister. This was a rural community and there were no other children within miles. One day after church, Helen went down to the river to play. She looked up to see a young girl her own age playing. "Hi," the girl said, "my name is Emily." Helen had no idea the young girl was from the *Spirit World*. She also did not know that two years before her own birth her mother had had a baby girl, named Emily, who died at birth. She mentioned her new friend to her father from time to time, but he was busy with other things. A year passed before he actually saw her playing and apparently talking to herself. Helen proudly made the introduction, "Daddy, this is Emily." Her father was horrified and outraged, repeating under his breath, "The devil, she is the devil."

The following Sunday he stopped the service and demanded that Helen approach the pulpit. "Kneel down," he told her. "Bow your head in shame." Before the altar and entire congregation, Helen knelt. "You have sinned. The devil has possessed your soul. Before you shall be welcomed into the house of the Lord, you must be purified and cleansed of your sins." He called for helpers from the congregation and motioned for them to lift her up and turn her upside down.

"The devil shall be gone from you. The devil shall be gone from you. Satan wears sheep's clothing to hide himself. You have sinned in the eyes of the Lord. Confess your sins now!" After what seemed to be an eternity, she was put down and went running out of the church sobbing uncontrollably.

She ran to the river where she had first met Emily. She sat weeping desperate and lonely tears. She thought, "My only friend has been taken away from me. I shall never see her again." She lifted her head to see Emily standing there.

"You didn't leave me, you didn't leave me," Helen wept.

The young girl, whom only Helen could see, replied, "Don't worry, I'll never leave you. I'll be here when you need me." Emily served as Helen's contact within the *spirit world* when Helen became a medium.

Now Helen was asking me, "How long have you been able to talk to the *spirit world*?"

"As long as I can remember," I replied.

"You know you have the calling, the gift to help others?" This was more a statement than a question.

"Thanks, but I really only want to compose music."

"Those who have the gift are called to do the work. God will find a way for what no man expects."

I remember feeling vaguely honored, but uncomfortable, and deciding it was time to leave. I thanked her genuinely and left as soon as courtesy allowed. But I had learned something about what a medium was, and mediumship. At least this thing had a name.

Life improved. I was in school getting my music degree, and I was studying the *Spirit World* on the side. It became more and more comfortable for me to dance between the realms of music and the intensifying involvement with psychics, mediums, and metaphysics. I decided that maybe the message was I should combine both my work and my loves. One of my compositions included a symphonic score for a ballet based on the Tarot cards.

Two months before graduation, I received another message from the DPs, that once again I would be moving, this time back to New York. By that time, I considered myself a true Californian and had no desire to go back East. Nor was this in any of my career plans. Maybe I had heard the messages from *upstairs* wrong. I'd sit back and see what was on the agenda for me.

One month had gone by when a friend of a friend visited California. An avid lover of music and the arts, she felt I'd do much better in New York as a serious composer. She said she was traveling much of the time and offered to let me stay in her New York apartment indefinitely. I left right after graduation with little rationale for going.

I hadn't been in New York more than two weeks when old friends asked me if I would mind doing psychic sessions for them. At the time I wasn't fully aware that I could make conscious and clear connections to the DPs, so most of my sessions were not as a medium, but as a psychic.

Friends kept telling me I should be paid for what I was doing. I had very little money. So, I reluctantly said yes even though I was very uncomfortable. This was the first time I'd been paid; for me this meant stepping over the professional line. Accepting money also meant a different level of commitment and confronting a deep-seated conflict. Did I want to endure the ridicule, the derisive laughter, or the constant "show me" challenges, or, most important, did I want to commit to what I considered to be the enormity of the responsibility? This was the crossroads of my life. My friends had mixed feelings, but supported me; they let me know they believed in me now, even if they hadn't in the beginning, that my gift was special, and that with it I should help people. Also, I needed to make a living. I was a serious composer, but I didn't want to continue being a starving, serious composer.

I started doing sessions at street fairs for three dollars. One time there were so many people in line to see me that the police blocked off a parking spot for hours after the fair had closed. Clients began referring me to others, and I was invited to prestigious organizations and universities to lecture. It was odd and inspirational. Still, I remained in conflict. The work became intensely demanding. I continued to compose, mainly in dance and theater. There was very little money coming in from my music, but I loved it. However, the phone kept ringing off the hook with people wanting to consult me as a psychic.

One day in a session, quite unexpectedly, the dead folks started coming through even more strongly. They had acknowledged themselves before, but this time I finally understood that the interaction with them was my real work. I was in session with a client and I heard a name and began describing the dead person to my client. I remember that the images were incredibly clear. I gave the information back to the client, who abruptly replied, "You are describing my grandfather exactly, but he's been dead for 20 years." From then on a DP started showing up at every psychic session. There was always a DP wanting to come through and communicate to the living.

My work took on a different meaning and more responsibility. Within a very short time I started doing readings for groups. This was very different from working one-on-one, whether as a psychic or as a medium. Afterward, I would wake up with massive headaches and pull the pillows over my head until I could get out of bed. Following sittings, which I call séances, I couldn't do any private psychic sessions for days.

Finally, I began to understand Helen's words, "You have the calling." I theorized that God had given me the gift to help others until it came time for my music. Still, ambivalence always remained. Whenever I socialized, the usual question arose, "And what do you do for a living?" I would respond, "I'm a composer." Then one of my friends would come over, "This is Suzane, my friend who talks to dead people." I would be looked at strangely. Were things about to levitate or did I have a broom stashed away somewhere? This would be followed by four thousand questions that usually started with, "I don't believe in that stuff, but . . ." It was always there. I still kept telling myself, this is only temporary. Ten years later I was still saying, "This is only until . . ."

God and the dead folks have won. I've accepted my path and realized I do indeed have a gift.

I have looked into the eyes of a mother or father, a daughter or a friend, and I'm able to open the door where the lost loved one is and communicate to help both sides. That's a privilege, a gift and a source of great pride for me—and for my grandmother.

Chapter 3

Making Contact

What do the dead folks want to tell you?
They're fine. They love you.
Don't be afraid for them.
Stop being afraid yourself.
And HEAL . . .

A BREAKTHROUGH (WHAT I SUPPOSE THE
DPs would call it) came during one of my
psychic sessions with a young man. It
started out ordinarily enough, but in the
middle of my reading, the DPs started
pushing and pushing at me. Their intensity
was causing me to interrupt myself, and
stop abruptly, which disconcerted my
client. It disconcerted him even more
when I told him that four of his dead
relatives had something to say to him.

They were loud and clear, and I wondered if he was ready to hear what they had to say.

The DPs were now dominating all sessions. They came when asked, when they wanted, and quite often unexpectedly. They came before sessions, during sessions and afterwards, offering critique or to express their own frustrations. They seemed passionate and adamant about promoting healing with those still on *this side*. I found no reason to resist anymore. I came to realize that a consciousness obviously exists with or without the physical body. In terms of who we are, or what do the DPs see when they look back and make contact, is really not so much of a "looking back," as what I have come to consider their particular state of consciousness. We don't become something other than what we are when we make our transition, but because we don't have a physical body there is a much different state of consciousness.

In the physical form, we can obviously escape an awful lot. When we do not have the physical body, we do not have the same forms of escape. There seems to be a "speeding up" of consciousness.

Of course, there are always exceptions. So, it is not so much that the DPs are looking back, as it is that they don't have the same level of emotions that we have in the physical form. They also, obviously, don't carry all the physical difficulties that they had prior to their passing. They basically come to bring messages of reassurance that they are doing well, and often times, suggestions and information for those on *this side* in order to heal unresolved relationship issues. Let me make this clear. They come to offer assistance and most definitely not to make decisions for us.

They won't interfere with our paths. They realize that ultimately it is still *our* life.

Let me give you some examples.

On a radio show I did in Providence, Rhode Island a couple of years ago, a woman called in and wanted to *talk* through me to her father. What happened is that her father did not show up, her mother did. When I identified her, there was a dead silence (no pun intended) on the phone from the woman caller. After a continued few minutes of this, the woman suddenly blurted out over the radio, "That bitch!" She then shouted into the phone that her mother was still keeping her from her father. So, clearly here was an opportunity for her to deal with some issues about her mother. She wanted nothing to do with her, and so the conflict will continue to lurk.

❧ ❧ ❧

Recently I was taping a television special that dealt with people just released from jail—thieves, forgers, tough guys, but not hardcore criminals. The young man whose story most affected the television personnel was Michael, a Chicano in his late twenties, in jail for three years for burglary. He was now in a halfway house trying with the aid of social workers to put together a functioning life. A week earlier, his youngest brother had been killed.

Michael's brother, Joey, came through to me immediately and began showing me episodic flashes of cars racing. I didn't have a sheltered childhood; I knew what drag racing looked like. Michael was struggling with this whole experience, numb with grief at his brother's death and pretty much in disbelief at what I was trying to do. Finally, he admitted to me—to the TV cameras— that yes, his brother had been drag racing for a gang initiation. The same gang that, years before, Michael himself had been proud to join.

Michael's guilt was exacerbated by the family turmoil churning around him. His two older brothers were in jail. His mother had looked to him to be a role model for Joey, the youngest. Instead, he'd gone to jail himself and now his little brother was dead. It was his fault, his mother said, as she wept and shouted at him, saying she hated him for it.

Meanwhile, Michael had two small sons himself with a girlfriend. He didn't want to see them, couldn't focus; he was wrapping himself in regret and blame. Joey, in spirit, was a lot less harsh than his mother. He urged Michael to take care of those kids. And, he told Michael that he didn't want him to end up *there* with him by being like him. "I'm here, but you can get your life together. Those kids and Mom need you. You're the only one left who can do anything for our family."

Michael kept mumbling through the session, "Joey wants me to change, Joey wants me to change."

Joey did his part. The rest is up to Michael.

THOSE IN THE NEXT LIFE LOOK AT US NOW, BUSY IN OUR LIVES, refusing commitment, denying responsibility, throwing off blame like uncomfortable shoes because truth often *pinches*. And as a result, so much goes unhealed. This is something the DPs are reminded of instantly when they *cross over.* To a great extent—not fully, but more often than most of us realize—we are responsible for choosing our parents, our partners, our successes and our failures. Life doesn't just happen. It is a working script, always in rewrite.

We can make it better, but we have to recognize most of the choices were ours to begin with, so that resolutions and responsibilities are, quite literally, the tasks *we* have to live with. That's what caring DPs who have lived their lives—whether well or wrongly—now know, and are trying to tell us. They seem to be afraid we might not make it.

The voices I hear come from our own loved ones who have gone before us. They are taking time out from their own paths to reach back spiritually and touch us. They don't have to do that. They finished this lifetime's roles, and have the rest of their journey to get on with. But they are making the time, borrowing a moment from infinity to stop, ask us to listen, and ask us to let them help. The choice is ours. They come to remind us of something we know in our souls, and conveniently forget once we get caught up in the business of Life. We are co-creators of our journey. Life is a script, and we begin putting the pieces together before birth. Their work is finished here. *Ours* is yet to be done.

ONE EVENING, DURING A GROUP SESSION, I WENT INTO FULL trance for the first time. I was sitting with the session group, there and yet, not there. A spirit, Elizabeth, introduced herself to me, letting me know that she would help me from now on as my *control.* This was a very odd feeling, amidst the odd feelings in general. Imagine being in a room with a great many dead people—and that is difficult enough to imagine—and they are talking to me, through me, but someone else is directing them, telling them to take turns. When I "came to," the session group fell over each other in their eagerness to tell me what had happened. They explained that my voice had changed, and so did my mannerisms. They said I was like a different person. They were ecstatic. Me? I had a headache the size of California.

Elizabeth, I am happy to say, has remained with me since that time and I have come to rely on her with gratitude. Traditionally, most mediums align themselves with someone in the *spirit world* who acts like a moderator by connecting both realms. I don't know much about Elizabeth's background when she was alive. She's quite private about that. (Arthur Ford, a renowned American medium several decades ago, did actually know his control. Fletcher, the control, and Arthur grew up together. Fletcher had died, I believe in World War I, and when Arthur discovered his abilities, Fletcher arrived to help him out.) The control and medium must have a reciprocity and mutual respect. For example, I think I have a great sense of humor, so I would have to be linked with someone else who could laugh a little. With Elizabeth, some of the details of our heritage are similar: my lineage is English and Irish, while Elizabeth is a bit more Scottish. I have a strong sense of what she looks like. Interestingly enough, she is similar in build to my paternal grandmother. I didn't choose her either, she chose me. She told me that means the upstairs unit decided we were a good match.

After that, I gave in to the DPs career plans for me. It seemed God had given me two gifts, the ability to contact the dead and the ability to compose music. Only one seemed to be able to pay the rent. I had devoted half my life to music, and still couldn't make a living at it. Who could figure? I knew, of course, who could figure. The DPs could. They wanted me to be a medium, and they wanted me to reconcile with my own family. They did not come straight out and tell me that, but the work I was doing with other families and their DPs had created some chinks in my armor against my own family. My mother had come to see me at one point, but I had not seen my father in five or six years. It was time.

When I did meet my father again, I saw a man on whom pain had taken its toll. By now, I felt more sadness toward him than anger, and I found there were many things I still admired about my dad. In the end, his end, we were lucky. He worked hard to become closer to his daughters, and we ultimately learned to love him. He had only a few more years to live after we reconciled, and in his last months, I could see that he wanted to die. He loved us, but he no longer wanted to be here. It wasn't an issue of suicide, he was simply ready to die. I also knew he'd be happier with his mother—my fat, huggable grandmother of so long ago.

Again, something in my personal life touched on my work as a medium. I knew my father wanted to go, to die, and I let him go, with my prayers, and sorrow for the man he might have been. I had a deeper understanding of his pain, the unbearable loss from which he could never himself move out of or let go. There are so many intertwinings, one person's pain, another's abandonment, one's anger, another's loss. The best you can do is understand the effect—both positive and negative—on your own life, and recognize it when you see it in others, and try to help them heal.

In so doing, I believe you begin to heal yourself. As a medium, I have helped others, and I have felt the healing in my own soul.

I consider myself a clairaudient—a trance medium.

For a while, I felt I had to be either psychic or medium. What's the difference? Let me start with this explanation. (This is like explaining the difference between an ophthalmologist and an optometrist.) When information comes in "psychically" the mind functions like a receiver, tuning into specific frequencies. Each psychic tunes into particular vibrations or frequencies in various ways. Those ways are as diverse as the individual psychics. Some psychics do and some don't acknowledge the *Spirit World*, and those that do have communication, may not be connecting with the spirits of specific deceased relatives of specific living people. Mediums do. There are psychics who do not work as mediums and there are mediums who do not work as psychics. Like me, there are those who do both.

The modern term for intermediating between both worlds is called *channeling*. I am sure that most of you have heard about channelers. One of the most recognized has been Jane Roberts, who was a channeler for *Seth*, which ultimately resulted in what is known as *The Seth Material*. In September 1963, the entity, Seth, first contacted Jane, resulting in Jane's mind rapidly flooding with new ideas and ending in "awakening" to herself in the process of automatic writing. Channelers deal with entities that usually contact them.

Mediums, who often have "controls" (like Elizabeth for me), work to channel those who have crossed over. I do want to say that Elizabeth comes through much stronger when I am working with groups. When working one-on-one with someone, it pretty much is the DP, myself and that person. I tend to "drop in" a trance-like state more when working in séances. This is where Elizabeth acts more as the control.

It is important that you understand when I act as a channel for a DP, that I am trying to receive and convey the messages, symbolism, and images they are giving me. This gives reason as to why sometimes it may appear that those of us who do this work are *grasping* for words. You must keep in mind that we have never met these DPs before. They are not familiar to us. We don't know them until that moment. Therefore, we don't know how they are going to come through or how they wish to make themselves known to a person in the room.

As a clairaudient or trance medium, I *hear* what the DPs are saying. I can also catch a whiff of a favorite perfume, a prized cigar, the acrid aroma of the two-pack-a-day smoker. And now and then, I can see the DP visitor fully. I often feel how death happened, not the pain, but the real physical pressure of a heart attack, a congested lung, or a cancer that spread and spread.

It can be a flawed process, for I am not always sure who is coming through, or the precise meaning of what they say. What I know is that the DPs are relentless about getting through and will absolutely stay with something until the particular person in the room "gets it." Someone I think most of you know, and many of you have seen is

John Edward of the television show *Crossing Over*. When a DP gets his attention, they will not let go until the person they have come to *visit* gets the message. I am sure you have noticed that John has long since given up trying to move on to something/someone else when a DP wants to "come through." It can lend to a frustration level on the part of the medium, the DPs, and the living, that make the experience quirkily entertaining beyond the standard revelations-by-a-medium book.

Communicating with the DPs is not like holding a normal conversation. I can't just ask them questions and get back answers in complete, cohesive sentences. Sometimes I just receive a word or even a strong physical sensation. It's no doubt because of my musicianship and affinity for music that the messages I receive are primarily auditory. I'll hear the sound of a name or a relationship or some other identifying characteristic. I have no idea what they might mean, so as I receive them and convey them to the sitters in the room, it's up to each person there to make the connection. Sometimes the DP will think he or she is giving the most significant identifying information, but if the person he's trying to reach simply isn't "getting it," another DP connected to that person will step in and offer further validating data to clear up the confusion.

I also "see" in my mind's eye, so to speak, visual images, such as a man in uniform or a small child in a red dress, or a young woman with blond hair. Very often, the image of a particular pet lying or running around close to one of the DPs is just the validating piece of information someone in the room needs to assure him or her that this DP "belongs" to them.

We all get *messages* from the Afterlife. How we receive them can vary greatly from person to person. We all receive information differently. This can be key to the process. And sometimes, I have had people contact me after a sitting or seminar with information or insight they have had. This was the case of the woman below.

A few years ago a woman, Beth, wrote to me about an experience she had during a seminar. In my seminars, I do an exercise designed to encourage people to trust, to open the door to their own contacts. She did on this occasion, and here's what she told me happened.

> During the exercise, a flabbergasted Beth was confronted with her father, who had been dead for many years. She had five other siblings. When Beth was a child, every Friday night her father would come home from work and get drunk. Her mother would rush the children out of the house until the father passed out. When she shepherded them back in a few hours later, the doors were always locked, and they had to crawl in through the windows. This had embittered Beth her whole life. Her father had locked them out. Beth, in turn, locked him out of her life.

> When her father came to her in spirit at the seminar, she was so surprised. She asked him the question that had bothered her for so many years. "Why did you lock us out of the house when you were drunk?"

> Beth's father replied, "When I'd wake up after passing out, I was still in a daze. I thought you were all asleep upstairs. I would make sure all the doors were locked so everyone was safe."

T<small>HIS</small> <small>MOMENT NOT ONLY RADICALLY CHANGED</small> B<small>ETH'S LIFE, BUT</small> it gave her a new relationship with her father. We live in our own perceptions, and our perceptions become realities. The DPs help us find truths we never knew.

Once we get a "message," it is imperative that we listen. That is our responsibility: to listen, be open, trust and know we are and have been in communication with our loved ones. It is our DPs' responsibility to get us the message, through whatever means possible—dreams, séances, etc. They even resort to contacting neighbors, our co-workers, and the children next door. They are very determined. It is to do them honor, to respect their devotion to us, and it is one of the primary motivations in my work. It's because my grandmother came so long ago to comfort me, and the "man in my room" told me that he would always protect me, that I can bring the messages of the DPs to other people now without fear. I can also tell you that the "man in my room" has kept *faith* with me all these years. His name is Tish. In life he was a school-teacher, and he helps me now in my seminars.

For each of us, this connection is different. The door to the other world became available to me through music. It's odd. When I was younger, I wanted my music to take people to another world. One day I thought about this and what I had wanted to do with my life. I realized that this is, in fact, what I do now. I introduce people to another world—to the place where their loved ones are. I didn't plan it like this, but ultimately, I ended up accomplishing my goal. Just *not* in the way I imagined it.

The question a medium is asked first by the living is, "Is my [husband, mother, child, friend, etc.] safe and happy?" The *unspoken* question is, "And when I die, will *I* be safe and happy?" This is understood by those in the *Afterlife.* They respond with positive support. In the last few years, however, the contacts and conversations have taken a new tangent. The DPs, who have had time—time plus—to think about things, believe the living need to hear some hard truths.

For many reasons, some individual, some universal, those who have left life before us are demonstrating a need to teach us about life while we're in it. Their messages are not about themselves, but urgently, about us. They want to tell us how to be happy in this life. That does not equate to how to be safe in this life. Safety, risk-free security is not what life is about.

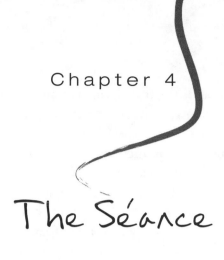

Chapter 4

The Séance

ALTHOUGH BY NOW, TALKING TO DEAD folks is, for me, a totally "natural" experience, I realize that for many of you, it must still seem like anything but that. So, I'd like to try to explain by example in this chapter, as clearly as possible, what it is that happens when I hold a séance. I also hope this helps you realize that because you're bound to them by love, you too, have the power to communicate with your loved ones who have passed.

A *séance* refers to a gathering in which phenomena such as telepathy and communication with the dead takes place. A séance does not have so much of the mysterious and exciting background that we have been led to believe. It actually stems from one of the translations of an old French word, *seoir*, which means to sit. In French, as well as in English, the word came to be used specifically for a meeting of people to receive spiritualistic messages. The first records of the use of the word séance can be found around the mid-1800s in French and English having to do with coming together for exciting spiritual meetings. For me, séance and sitting are interchangeable. I usually refer to the gatherings in which I am involved in as s*essions*. In my séances, I usually drop into a trance-like state wherein my guide, Elizabeth, takes control and monitors the DPs for me. That's why I have come to refer to myself as a transmedium or trance-medium.

I remember one long ago dinner in particular that was to include a session. The description of the séance during this evening will also present the informal agenda of a sitting: the negativity and skepticism before the session, the spiritual "Grand Central Station" during, and the explosive joy afterward. I'm the last person to arrive at a séance. The dead folks make sure it happens that I way. It also gives me an opportunity to share with you how I work.

Because I'm going to be using my mind to "tune-in" quite literally to a frequency that is quite different from the one we use for everyday verbal communications, it's necessary for me to begin to "tune-out" of that earth-bound frequency several hours in advance. By the time I am set to leave for a session, I've been in an altered state preparing for hours.

My body and mind are aware that I'll be tapping into another dimension where the DPs are. The sequencing has already begun, and throughout my day, my intuition has been switching on to high, logic to low. It all has to do with entering or aligning my mind with vibrations from another plane. Energy creates vibrations (and remember that energy never dies), but different energy levels create different vibrations. While we're on this plane, we're in our physical bodies, which are dense and therefore lower the vibrations that emanate. When we cross over and shed our physical bodies, those vibrations rise to a faster, higher frequency, which is why most people aren't able (or think they aren't) to tune into them.

In order to make contact with the DPs, I have to raise the frequency of my vibrations and they, because they want to communicate, have to lower theirs. We do this until we are both effectively tuned-in to the same frequency. I am, in effect, acting as the radio receiver; receiving signals and broadcasting them to my clients.

As the time of the séance comes closer, my right brain will have taken over. My left brain retains precisely enough control for specific, short-term, goal-oriented functions, like driving. I usually drive to séances carefully. That is the calm part.

As I arrive, and start walking towards the door, the adrenaline starts pumping.

I try to collect my wits, relax my tense shoulders, take a last deep breath, and concentrate on thinking strong, positive thoughts.

And then, I hit the *wall*.

The Wall

The *wall* is located a few feet beyond the host or hostess who is welcoming me at the door, and a few feet in front of the guests. It is the projection from these assembled guests and their collective negative emotions. The *wall-builders*, fear and anxiety, arrived well before me. They have come with the people who are waiting to see just what will or will not happen. Fear asks them, "What am I doing here? She has to be a fraud, doesn't she? Will my dead relatives really show up? What if they're in some place horrible, like Hell? What if I break down and cry and look ridiculous? If any of this is real, what does it mean about me, about my own death?"

Anxiety maintains the sweat glands, the nervous laughter, the studied aloofness, and the many, many bad jokes. The word *séance* triggers defensive psycho-physiological responses; the stigma of "stupidity" at best to "sin" at worst, and intimations of sulphur and foreboding. People's antipathies and stereotypes do dramatically change after going through the séance experience.

I know this change will occur eventually, but I have to contend with the negative emotions almost immediately because they confront me with that wall of extreme resistance and denial. Breaking down resistance is more difficult than breaking down the *Walls of Jericho*. It is imperative for me, with the help of the dead folks, to get through to the living with specific information so we can all work together to achieve the best possible communication.

Everyone has a vague idea that the process is like doing a search on the Internet and up comes the answer. *Wrong.*

For example, dead folks may come through me belonging to someone who never knew them, never heard of them. Perhaps it is a great-grandparent who passed over when a great-grandchild was young or not yet born. When this happens at a séance there's a big fuss; the dead person insists they belong to the living person, and the living person has no idea who they are, but the DP won't give up. The dead folks will keep my mind under siege until they feel a proper connection is made.

Another example: Some frightened person wants to attend a session, but doesn't want to go alone, so he or she drags along a reluctant friend or relative. The friend or relative sits there thinking, "I'm nuts for coming, this is all ludicrous," when suddenly, without warning, one of his own relatives from the DPs comes through. The reluctant guest goes into shock or complete denial and can't talk. Meanwhile, the DP is frustrated. I'm even more frustrated.

People hold on to hate, too, not just to love or to mourning. If someone hated the DP, he or she will refuse to admit who the DP is. There are a great many examples of that. Scary.

Someone being truly disrespectful, with a "prove it" attitude will most likely produce a negative effect on how much information I'll get. This is a *wall* I expect, but get very tired of. Those in spirit want little more than to let you know they're fine and still love you. You resist, put up the *wall*, and you lose. I may get tired, but in the end, *you* lose.

We're All Here

Six to twelve people are to attend this séance. Fewer are always easier for me. Everyone will have someone come through, and who *receives* more is out of my control. Sometimes the DPs stop by only to let you know they're around. Consider how many dead friends or relatives (including unknown ones) a single living person may have, and multiply that by the number of people in the group. All of the dead folks are determined to push through, through me, and reach all of the attendees, some of whom are determinedly denying the whole experience. I can sense a large number of DPs present this evening. A major sorting, pushing and pulling, tug of war is going on, and the séance has not officially started yet. This is where the help of my *control*, Elizabeth, is greatly appreciated. Oh, yes, she is there also.

These are the thoughts the hostess had as I entered the room that she shared with me later. She had no idea I was processing the *Wall*.

Suzane arrived and it was obvious to me that she was not all there. Something about her inability to concentrate on the here and now. She could answer questions and tell us how to proceed and what to expect, but she was clearly, for lack of a better description, totally preoccupied or maybe just occupied. This heightened my nervous anxiety considerably. I needed this person to be in control and I was not sure that she was.

The woman sitting next to me was very anx-ious to have some sort of ecstatic experience. She had been to a séance before and her first husband came through. She wanted to feel him once again, this time without her present husband being there.

— Faith

The Rules

"There are rules to a séance," I announce to the group, "and the first rule is the dead folks want you to put out your cigarettes so we can get started."

No Smoking

Actually it's me who is affected by working in a smoke-filled room. At least half of the DPs, themselves, smoked while alive and it's quite common for the attendees to smell smoke during a séance if the relatives coming through were smokers. Olfactory clues are among the most prevalent during a session, especially clearly definable aromas such as flowers, perfumes, and tobacco. People's pets come through too, often making an aromatic appearance.

Smells are not the only format for animals; generally they'll be lying or pacing in front of the attendee they are connected to. I can't remember a séance when at least one dog, cat, or bird hasn't demanded attention. During one sitting in South Dakota, I saw a horse and a pig in spirit standing in the middle of the room. When I announced the animals' presence, one woman joyfully claimed them as her pets. The woman sitting next to her was extremely relieved to learn that the odors she smelled and the tail she felt waving in her face were in fact really there.

NO DRUGS OR DRINKING

I'm responsible for the séance and for what happens. Everything that happens is filtered through me, literally. I'm working very hard to make information clear. Each person needs to be as sharp as possible to recognize and assimilate the information.

This particular rule developed because of some not-so-positive experiences. Back in my early days, a student of mine asked me as a favor to do a séance for a friend on Halloween. *Halloween.* That by itself should have warned me. The friend really wanted the session, but others there didn't. It was very disorganized and very tense. To bolster his own confidence, I suppose, the friend had decided to get very soused and continued gulping beer during the evening. He waited while I made contact, listened, walked around, wobbled, and suddenly fell on top of me, smashing my bare feet on the way down. I abruptly came back into consciousness, without having a clue as to what had just happened, other than being aware of the intense pain in my feet and this guy on top of me. I couldn't do séances for six months afterward.

This leads to a third rule.

NEVER TOUCH A MEDIUM WHILE IN A TRANCE.

You can break the contact. You can also break the medium.

Sit in a Circle, and Stay There.

We sit in a circle and no one can leave the circle until the séance is completed. No, you don't have to sit holding hands as was done in the old days, or as in the movies, but you can't leave. I advise people at the beginning: if you are not in the mood to talk to your dead folks, this is not the place to be. Leave now or you're here for the duration. No one has ever left.

The Right Chair, in the Right Place.

I pace around the room in a circle to find the right place to sit. I've always wondered why dogs behave this way. I do it when sessions take place at someone else's house. For me it involves polarity; placement in the right direction, usually north or west. The chair must be hard and straight-backed, since I shift around continually throughout the séance.

Lighting

The last rule involves a prop, which is a red bulb. It serves two functions. One reason being that people don't want to feel they are being put on the spot or stared at. The red bulb will dim and soften the room, giving people a sense of privacy. The second reason for the bulb is to help the living to possibly see the emanation or presence of their relatives in spirit. One can't see the *spirit world* in bright lights. In fact, what most people do report seeing are faint white, blue, or indigo lights around me or other people in the room.

THERE REALLY AREN'T ANY OTHER DEFINITE RULES, AND NONE of the above involves *setting* the stage or an atmosphere. They're important to the welfare of everyone who is attending. This should be a joyous and exciting experience, a connection with loved ones who have passed over into the *spirit world*. In order for these connections to happen, each person must know his or her part and take responsibility for it. This applies not only to the medium, but to all of us. We're in this together.

The Séance Begins

The last step of preparation, which is actually the first step of the séance, is the recitation of a prayer out loud. I choose either the Lord's Prayer or the Twenty-third Psalm, which is given below.

> *The Lord is my Shepherd; I shall not want.*
> *He maketh me to lie down in green pastures;*
> *he leadeth me beside the still waters.*
> *He restoreth my soul. He leadeth me in the*
> *paths of righteousness for his name's sake.*
>
> *Yea, though I walk through the valley*
> *of the shadow of death,*
> *I will fear no evil; for thou art with me;*
> *thy rod and thy staff comfort me.*
> *Thou preparest a table before me*
> *in the presence of mine enemies;*
> *thou anointest my head with oil;*
> *my cup runneth over.*

Surely goodness and mercy
shall follow me all the days of my life,
and I will dwell in the house
of the Lord for ever.

With the prayer, the session officially begins. The room is dimly lit. My eyes will be closed until it's over. I feel the presence of everyone waiting, hopeful, excited, apprehensive. I hear myself saying the end of the prayer, and the voices of others in the room repeating the words with me. As the voices and those beautiful words recede, I feel the presence of Elizabeth. She takes over, becoming stronger, and my voice, or the voice she uses, becomes louder, faster, laced with an Irish-Scottish brogue.

Meanwhile, as Elizabeth and I settle in, the DPs are with us, waiting to get through. They have so much to say. I feel myself bombarded by different names coming from different directions and different DPs, each demanding my attention, each asserting the right to be heard first. I hear their names, at least four or five at the same time, each pulling, each directing me to the place where "their" living person is seated. The strongest, most determined souls are the ones who bulldoze their way through to be the first "on line." Why? They were that way when they were alive! This isn't to imply that the shy, reserved types don't get a shot at it, just that the pushy ones get there first.

My relatives were the last to show up, some-
thing the rest of the group noticed too. Some of
them were worried that I did not know any dead
people? I was getting a bit nervous and jealous as

relatives of all the other people kept showing up and none showed up for me.

Relatives on my father's side seemed much stronger in spirit than those on my mother's side. My father's father was very strong, yet I didn't really know him. He died in 1968.

The funniest exchange came when my two grandfathers argued about who gave me my creativity. My father's father seemed to give in to my mother's father and then said I get my bad teeth from that side of the family, too.

— Michael

Elizabeth ensures that everyone on the DP side gets a chance. No one is left out and she controls the demonstrative ones from completely dominating the séance. This is difficult, but we always work it out.

Meanwhile, on the side of the living, it takes a while for people to loosen up and to understand the way I speak with the accent and rapid-fire delivery.

Dark and quiet, the room was black but for the light of a red bulb and two candle flames. We sealed our circle with the Lord's Prayer and sat in silence.

At first, Suzane moved around a lot, fidgeting, adjusting her position, rubbing her feet on a faded floor pillow.

Then, bellowing out, Suzane/Elizabeth started calling out names: "I'm hearing a J name on my left. A John, or could it be James." (My grandfather is John.) "A P name, Paul." (That's my brother.)

"H, *a female. Sounds like Hazel.*" (That was my mother's aunt.)

She never mismatched relatives to participants or failed to delineate intricate family relationships [i.e., a father's second wife's daughter's child].

It was *like the DPs were having a party "up there" and* we *were gathered "down here." Suzane* was *the go-between attending at both gatherings, and relaying the events of theirs to us.* We *heard accounts of our relatives interacting with one another* in *ways that were characteristic of them from their time on earth. Shem's father made french toast; James's grandfather, the fireman, repeatedly complained that Jean's grandfather, the lumberjack,* was *smoking.*

Later dogs, cats, and birds—the DPets—*came through, and confirmed their presence by acting* in *ways characteristic of their earth-plane behavior. My mutt, Skippy, true to* his *feisty personality, flirted with the* dog *next to him and picked fights with the bigger dogs.*

— Naomi

Identification

This process is going to sound confusing, and it is confusing to go through. I have learned to accept it all, but it remains frustrating.

Communication with DPs does not happen in the same way as we know it. I cannot just ask a direct question and get a direct answer. It would be much easier for everyone on both sides, and for me in the middle if I could, but it just doesn't happen that way. In the first place, communication is not always spoken in sentences. I may only hear a word or receive a very strong physical sensation.

I'm a medium and a musician, and for me, sound is the dominant sense. When I'm connecting and aligning myself with the *spirit world*, the *sound* of the name or names I can hear are crucial to the connection. Identifying a member of the Dead People's Society can only be done by the living person to whom they are connected. Sometimes the DP will give his or her name, initial, or even middle name, or give the name of someone else related to them, either living or dead. The name or certain sound that makes the contact easier and clearer from the DP's perspective will be the one I will generally hear first but it may mean nothing to the living.

The sounds may differ from the actual letter. I might hear the name *John,* which can be Sean or Juan or Johann. The sounds of *Sh* or *Ch* are similar and *IL* or *EL* may sound the same, as do other letters and sounds. If there are two *Johns* in spirit at a séance, I'll hear a third DP connected to one of them giving additional information to clear up any confusion. People are concerned I won't be able to make contact if, for example, their relative didn't speak English. Don't worry. I can, but I will still hear the information only in English. Somewhere "up there" is a cosmic decoder.

Information is neither literal or linear. If I hear the word *mother,* it could mean mother or mother-in-law or mother's side of the family. *Sister* could mean sister or sister-in-law. If the client is a man, my first perception may be that I'm receiving information from his mother when in fact I'm receiving information from his wife's family, because there are things the dead folks want his wife to know. He may not care, but they're going to tell him anyway.

For a woman, *father* may be her husband or someone from her husband's side of the family. And it doesn't stop at marriage. Relationships of all sorts are package deals and a variety of connections are identified. Sometimes the clues to determine identity seem to be purposefully vague, as the DP discovers that although he or she may want to reach the client, it is not what the client wants or needs.

I agree this isn't logical. I didn't make the rules. This is all related to time spans from the DPs' point of view, multiple connections in varying lives. They have to lower their frequencies to connect through me. I raise mine to receive them. (To explain how to "tune in" to the frequency level, the best analogy is the ability of dogs, dolphins, and other animals to hear sounds and frequencies that the human ear cannot.) We're all doing the best we can!

The DPs love to have their talents and gifts acknowledged. When this happens they'll hold up their hands for me to see or I may actually feel in my own hands the physical sensation of their gifts; for example if they sewed, worked with wood, or played an instrument.

I will also feel certain physical conditions that DPs might have had immediately prior to their deaths as well as certain physical illnesses; pressure in my chest or a pushing sensation from someone who may have had a heart attack. For lung disease or breast problems there is a heaviness in my chest and restricted breathing. Any such sensation occurs very quickly and then is gone.

Sometimes I may get a sense of distance if they lived abroad. If I sense distance but the living person says, "Oh no, they lived right here," then I know it's an emotional distance. Which is sad.

More Walls

There's always a reason why some DPs show up and others do not. I don't always know why but I believe that a *Higher Power* does. In a full séance, the size of the group may be a factor. This is why much of my work is done privately. For some, recovering from the immediate shock of the contact and the time it takes to admit to the contact, it's a delayed process. Often there are circumstances which are still so emotional or difficult that the living cannot handle the presence of the loved one who is now in spirit. The negative emotions are the hardest: despair, hatred, fear, rage, envy, frustration, self-pity. It's a long list.

I've had clients who won't acknowledge half- or step-siblings because they felt cheated emotionally or financially by the parents. There have been daughters and sons who were molested by a now dead family member or other relative, who are still legitimately very angry. If we, the living, still cannot handle the emotions of jealousy, resentment, or intense hate, this resistance will stop or hinder the communication.

One of the hardest things to acknowledge is that we feel *abandoned* when a loved one dies. Sometimes the living relative sits in front of me stiff with anger and sorrow, unable to admit to that feeling of abandonment. The DP then cannot come through clearly. I know what is happening but I can't intervene. Another client may deny the DP ever existed for reasons I will never know.

I am not the judge of who must be heard or who must hear. Eventually, the DP will realize the futility and let go, realizing that what he or she needs to say to the living cannot be said in this place or time. The bottom line is this: people only believe, hear, or accept what they want to.

When The Walls Come Down

When it all comes together there will be joy and delighted recognition and tears. Tears that come from the contact with the loved one in spirit. Tears of freedom; the freedom of letting go.

The thought of talking to dead relatives made me uneasy. My mother had died almost 20 years before and I just was not at all sure I wanted to dredge up all that pain and have a conversation with her.

At the age of 16, I had woken up one snowy February, in 1973, in the top bunk of my bed at boarding school, knowing that my mother was dead. I didn't know how she died; she hadn't been sick or anything, and I didn't know how I knew, but I knew. My mother was killed in a car accident that February night long ago. And I still have no idea how I knew. When Suzane got to me, my mother came through immediately and the first thing she said through Suzane was, "I visited you once before." I knew at that instant that long ago my mother had come herself to tell me *that she was dead.* I was safe and warm in her love. And without hesitation or thought I said, "Yes, I know."

— Faith

❧ ❧ ❧

I decided the best course of action was to surprise my husband with the séance. No sense letting the man think I had gone completely crazy. His grandfather had been a very influential person in Brian's life, and I knew Brian would attend in the hope of getting a message from his grandfather.

His *grandfather asked how Brian had gotten* [his] *watch, was it directly given to him after* [the grandfather's] *death or was it given to Brian's dad first?* Brian's answer was choked with emotion as he replied that his mother had given it to him directly after his father's death.

A watch? This was news to me. We are married 24 years, and I never knew he had this watch.

— Lois

❧ ❧ ❧

Many surprising things happened that evening, but the one event that stands out in my mind most involved a woman present, Mrs. A, whose son I had gone to high school with ten years earlier. The boy had died at the age of 15, but I don't remember if the cause of his death was ever made absolutely clear. Mrs. A was a confirmed atheist and she was participating in the séance, as she claimed, out of curiosity.

She seemed to be rather amused by the whole thing. The séance began with a circle of chairs and the Lord's Prayer. There was no sitting around a table holding hands like so many movies I had seen. No raps on the table or odd noises. No candles blowing out. Although I remember feeling nervous, I didn't feel afraid; rather, there was a sense of peace in the room.

Finally, Suzane addressed Mrs. A. She told her that she was surrounded by three male figures who had passed on to the "other side." One was a father vibration of the name Arthur. Mrs. A's father's name was in fact Arthur. Suzane saw a dog at her feet and described a former family dog. Mrs. A's face no longer looked amused. When Suzane mentioned a young boy around the age of 15, a son vibration, Mrs. A began to cry.

"He is small for his age, with black hair. He wants to tell you that it wasn't the drugs that killed him, but that it was his time to go and that he is at peace. He also wants to thank you for not throwing out the stuffed walrus."

There were more details to the message that I have forgotten with time but I can't forget the look on Mrs. A's face. Afterward, she told us that weeks *prior to the séance, she had gone into her son's room, sat on the bed, and held his toy walrus, wondering whether to continue keeping it. She had put it back on the bed and left the room, closing the door behind her.*

— Janet

The Séance Is Ending

At this point I am exhausted. Elizabeth is telling me that it's now time for her to leave. I must return to my body fully. The DPs are still present but there is a sense that it is time to close the door. I thank them for coming and many people in the group thank them as well.

There have been heartaches but there is a lot of laughter and joke telling as well during the séance. You didn't think they would lose their sense of humor "over there," did you? In many cases the dead are more lively than the living! The group laughs with them and often at themselves. The group relaxes, because laughter is wonderful and relaxing. Fear and anxiety cannot stand up to laughter, and they ooze away.

The séance takes place in a natural progression, never more than two to two and one-half hours. I will have gone around the entire circle and it will now be time for questions or to ask for a DP who may not have shown up. If the DPs are too distant to pick up information it's because they are not "on line" or not meant to come through at this time. Within moments I feel myself gradually coming back as Elizabeth fades. I separate from those in spirit slowly, announcing to the living, "You can put the lights back on. Slowly, please."

I prefer people to be still and not smoke, but that's tough after what they've been through, so I just let it slide. It will be several hours before I return to my normal non-altered state of consciousness. Meanwhile, I need to present a semblance of polite attentiveness, so I've learned to interact, not always very well, but enough to handle brief conversations.

This is hard work; it is exhausting, confusing, and exhilarating. I don't walk into walls anymore or get headaches the morning after. It does get better with time. Most of all, however, despite my exhaustion, I'm always left with a sense of gratitude for the gift and the privilege I've been given to help these people answer some of the questions that may have been haunting their lives and preventing them from arriving at a resolution with the past and moving on with the learning they have yet to do.

Chapter 5

Tell Him Yourself; He'll Hear You

"FRANK!" I HEAR THE NAME FRANK IN my inner ear as I align with Elizabeth. The group is small: three men and two women sitting quietly and uneasily, waiting for the medium to get started. As she and I align, I talk faster and louder, especially at the beginning as I connect with those members of the DPs coming through. I ask God that, with His permission, loved ones in spirit may make their presences known to me.

"FRANK!"

The man in spirit demanding to be recognized appears physically strong, in his fifties. Standing next to him is a younger man in a uniform, but his spirit is fading as the energy in the spirit of the stronger, older man pushes him into the background. He will have to wait until later to be heard.

"A man named Frank," I tell the group, "in his fifties. And there's someone else younger . . . No, he's gone now."

Joe, the man sitting next to me, says that Frank had been his uncle.

"It feels as though he's on your mother's side of the family," I continue.

"Yes."

Frank tells me that Joe's mother was his younger sister. He speaks boldly, his manner almost arrogant, of his looks and flare for the ladies. Four times he had been married but he had only one child, a daughter Amy, to whom *Joe* had been very close. Amy and Joe were the same age and both were only children, *friends as well as cousins,* says Frank.

"I was a better father than husband," Frank concedes. He was glad that Amy's mother remarried. Too bad that the new man was not as spicy as himself, but he was more secure, a husband who didn't drink or gamble. I repeated this to Joe.

Joe agrees, nods his head, "It's all true."

The young man in uniform suddenly comes back. He's trying to make himself known to me but he's confusing me. I thought he belonged to Joe but no, he indicates it's Beverly, Joe's wife. The young man says his death was quick, from an accident involving a vehicle of sorts. As I link my thoughts with his to find out more information, I'm abruptly overwhelmed by the smell of smoke, smoke from a fire, not a cigarette or pipe. The smell permeates all my senses, making it impossible to ignore the spirit connected to the smoke. Again the young man in uniform must wait; this new presence needs to be acknowledged now.

I hear the name *Dana,* and as I concentrate on the vibration I become aware it belongs to a young girl. She seems to be around the age of nine or ten, and lying next to her is a large dog. As our thoughts entwine she lets me know that she was related to the man sitting across from me, Edward. The connection is her mother, Dana says. As I repeat all this aloud, Edward says nothing.

Dana continues: she had passed over from a fire but the fire wasn't in the house she lived in. To me, she seems to be insisting that she had been saved but had to go back into the house. The man across from me still says nothing. The information I'm getting from this little girl makes no sense to me but I will keep passing it on anyway. No one will respond; everyone sits completely silent.

The little girl in spirit stops talking. She waits and I wait. Finally, Edward speaks, unwillingly.

"Is Dana okay? Did she feel pain when she died?"

Dana, through me, promptly replies that she is very happy and felt no pain at the time of her death. She says that the smoke filled her lungs but she never felt the fire.

"Tell my mother I'm not alone and the sheep dog is here with me."

Edward says nothing more. Only after the readings were over did he tell me what had happened. He was Dana's uncle and she was his sister's daughter. Apparently, while she had been visiting at a neighbor's house, a fire broke out and she had been rescued through a window. She was safe, but when she realized that her dog was still upstairs in the house, she ran back while the house was still ablaze. By the time anyone realized she was gone, it was too late. She was found with her arms around her dog; both were dead.

In an unsteady voice, Edward said he would try to find a way to tell his sister about this. He hoped Dana's coming through might give some solace and comfort to his sister, who had never forgiven herself for her daughter's death.

Meanwhile, the young girl's presence has left the room heavy with emotion but we have to continue. It is early in the evening and there are more who want to make themselves known.

Sitting next to Edward is a tall, striking woman named Lauren. I hear clearly *husband* and again feel the presence of the man in uniform. First he had indicated Joe and then Beverly, now Lauren. Someone in the *spirit world* will move from one living person to another during a group reading only if the living persons are in some way connected.

This time the man's presence was much more vibrant, definitive. I align my thoughts with his and hear "Al . . . Alan . . . Alex."

"The same man in the uniform is here, connecting with you, and I hear a name sounding like Alan or Alex. I'm also hearing husband."

"That's Alan, my husband," Lauren replies. "He was a pilot."

Alan now comes through much stronger and his vibration is one of security and warmth. There is no doubt the man was this way when he was alive. He talks about his death, that he passed from an accident involving a motorcycle. He makes it clear the accident was not his fault, but rather someone else's carelessness. His last images were of being thrown in the air, whereupon he left his body immediately. As he talks through me, tears run down Lauren's face.

Gradually, Alan's great sense of humor and wit triumph over Lauren's tears. And he says he knows everyone. Everyone? Joe, Beverly, Edward, Lauren—could he be connected to the last man as well? Rather than trying to figure it out, I ask, "I think Alan is trying to tell me that he's connected in some way to all of you?" As I look quizzically around at the group, the last man, Sam, volunteers, "I was Alan's best friend and best man at his and Lauren's wedding."

I am still linked with Alan. I hear him then say sister. As I repeat this, with the words hardly out of my mouth, Beverly yells, "I'm Alan's sister." Continuing through me, Alan says that he had introduced Beverly to Joe. Beverly laughs, "I was dating a guy Alan didn't like and he kept insisting I go out with Joe. I can't believe this!"

Alan's last plug is that when Beverly and Joe have a son, they name the boy after him. Alan belongs to them all; even Edward had met him several times through his friendship with Joe. Alan hasfinally dominated the session and he is the link that brought all of them together.

Suddenly, another spirit. I am directed to go to Sam.

"I'm picking up mother. I'm feeling a heaviness in my chest as though she had difficulty breathing. I'm hearing cancer, did your mother have cancer?"

"Yes. She died of lung cancer."

"It feels as though your mom has been gone a long time. I'm getting a resonance of springtime. That must have been her birth or passing time because that's the way they identify themselves to me."

"My mother died in May, 15 years ago when I was 21," Sam says. "I graduated from college in May, the same month my mom passed away."

"She says your dad remarried. You've seemed to accept this more than your brother. She's says your brother still blames your father for her death."

"I know, but it wasn't his fault. I knew my father and mother were planning on getting divorced, but then my mother got sick. My brother was much younger and he didn't know about the divorce, so he felt my father caused her illness. My brother still won't talk about my mother's death and he doesn't have much to do with my father since she died."

"Your mother says she and your dad were just different people; it wasn't your dad's or anyone else's fault. She would like you to give your brother her love and asks if you could prompt your brother to deal with your dad while he's still alive. There won't be a rug big enough to shove all your brother's anger under if he doesn't deal with this while your dad is still alive."

Sam's mother still remains strong as Alan comes back once again. This time his focus is on Beverly and he's bringing forward another spirit.

"Besides Alan, I'm picking up a female vibration on your mother's side of the family. I believe an aunt or grandmother who had a stroke. Her name is either Dorothy or Dora, or someone to whom she was connected has that name."

"That was Dora, my grandmother, my maternal grandmother," Beverly replies.

"She says you were the only granddaughter."

"I was, everyone else had sons."

"She's holding something up like lace, or something she made with her hands."

"She embroidered."

"She says she left you something."

"Tablecloths and linens."

"She was there to help bring your brother over."

"My mother always said she was sure Grandma would have been there to greet Alan. I guess she was right."

Once again I feel Alan pulling me toward Lauren. "Lauren, Alan wants you to know that although he's not replaceable, you have a full life ahead of you and he wants you to share it with someone. I know this may sound strange, but he tells me you both talked about it."

"It's not strange at all," Lauren answers. "he always had this feeling he would go in a crash. Being a pilot, it was on his mind but it wasn't a plane that killed him. A foreigner on a motorcycle, who didn't see the red light." She is quiet for a moment. "He would always tell me he wanted me to remarry if he died."

Alan doesn't let that go by.

"Lauren," I said, "Alan wants you to know that when you are ready to reenter the marketplace, give him a call; he would love to help in the picking-out department!"

Now everyone has Alan stories; they all begin to reminisce. I'm exhausted, and I know it's near to the time for the door to close. I ask, "Are there any more questions, anything else to say?"

Beverly glances at Lauren and starts to ask, "Do you . . .?" Then she looks down at her hands in her lap and says how much she misses her brother who was her friend and confidant.

"Tell Alan I loved him."

I turn to her. "You can tell him yourself. He'll hear you."

This session was very special. Group readings where the resolution is filled with such warmth are a joy. Alan's meaningfulness to all the guests was the surprise element.

Chapter 6

Calling Home

It is also possible for me to hold a séance over the telephone: you're there, I'm here, and the DP is, somehow, with both of us. These séances can be even more touching, and more surprising, especially if they are not scheduled, especially if a DP shows up just as the phone starts to ring.

A few minutes before a noontime séance appointment, I can hear my phone start to ring and the answering machine click on. With that, a young man's presence in spirit permeates the room. Who is he? *J—Jim—James?* There are other DPs there too, but he is stronger. I can feel his determination to contact whoever is on the other end of my line.

"Suzane, this is Barbara Ann," the caller starts to leave a message. I don't know who she is, but I know a DP wants to contact her. Someone must have given her my phone number.

"Hello, hello, I'm here," I interrupt. "Just give me a minute to get the tape machine ready." (I always tape a phone session and send the tape to the caller. I don't keep them. I don't want to!)

"Barbara Ann, I wasn't expecting your call, but there's a young man in spirit here named *James* who wishes to give you his love and let you know he's okay."

I hear her gulp back tears.

"James . . . Jimmy is . . . *was* . . . my son."

"He's telling me that he passed from an accident of sorts but he insists that it happened through the carelessness of someone else. He's saying something like, you know the person he's talking about or you know *of* this person. I'm not getting this clearly, but he keeps repeating something about a legal matter or issues. I feel him saying there are legal matters pertaining to his death. He wants you to follow through and deal with them. He says, don't be afraid."

There is almost a hum of resistance at the end of the phone. Not the same resistance as when I'm being challenged about a contact, but something else. Barbara Ann seems frightened and unwilling to deal with the truth.

None of this seems to matter to James, he keeps reiterating that his mother must deal head on with this obviously touchy legal matter. It doesn't make sense, his persistence and his mother's equal resistance.

"I don't want to sound like a broken record, Barbara Ann, and my job is not to tell you what you should or should not do, but it is important you understand what I'm getting from *James*. He feels it's imperative for your financial future that you take legal action regarding his death. Your son wants to make sure you are taken care of, it's as if he planned to take care of you and now is no longer able to. Your son is quite headstrong! He wants you to be cared for."

"I understand," Barbara Ann answers slowly.

Suddenly, a bell goes off in my head and I finally realize that the legal situation must pertain directly to *James's* death. Barbara Ann has to be well aware of what I am trying to relay to her. But why does she seem too paralyzed to deal with the matter, unless she isn't strong enough emotionally? I will wait. I know she wants to ask something.

"Is *Jimmy* okay, can you tell him how much I miss him? How much I've worried if he's all right? And how much I love him?" I feel the devastation at the other end of my telephone.

"Barbara Ann, *Jimmy* is fine. You know, you can tell him yourself how much you love and miss him. We are only parted physically by death. We are heard and felt by the ones who love us."

I can hear Barbara Ann catch her breath to stop herself from responding.

"Umm, I don't want to pressure you, Barbara Ann, but James is pressuring me. Is it clear to you what he wants you to do?"

"Yes," Barbara Ann reluctantly replies. "Does he have anything else he wants to say?"

"I'm hearing a name with the letter H like Harold or Howard. Do you know who James is referring to?"

"Yes, his name is Harry, that's the man I've been seeing for several years. Jimmy liked him very much."

"James wants to thank Harry for helping you. Oh, he's saying legal again. Does that mean Harry is helping you legally or is he an attorney?"

"Yes, he is a lawyer and, yes, he'll help me with the case."

"Do you understand why James is so insistent that you follow through with the lawsuit?"

"Yes, it will be very difficult for me, but I understand."

Suddenly, another bell goes off in my head but this one is intense. The lawsuit must have something to do with James's father. I had *wondered* why James hadn't said anything about his father. Just as the thought passes through my mind, James starts to say, through me, "The legal matter is connected with my father."

The medium has to be cautious now. I don't want to say anything else. I can feel Barbara Ann's immediate withdrawal. Obviously, there's dangerous ground here.

This time the pause is so long I wonder if Barbara Ann might just hang up. Then she chokes out: "My ex-husband owns his own company. His business is installing skylights for large buildings. My son had spent his summers working for him to earn money for college. His business wasn't doing well so James—my ex-husband is also James—was in financial trouble, and was trying to cut costs. The law requires a certain number of safety bars to be installed in the work area. My ex-husband decided to keep using old bars, which were not up to code, and take the chance that they'd pass a spot inspection."

She pauses again, attempting to hold back the tears. "Please forgive me, I'm sorry. My son was standing on one of the bars when it cracked and broke. He fell 20 stories to his death."

There wasn't much else left to say.

"Barbara Ann, James is fine now, he just wants you to be cared for as he would have done. The money is only to take care of you, he doesn't hate his father. He says he understands this still has to be your decision."

"I'm still in shock. I wake up night after night thinking this was just a bad dream. That my son will walk through the door again. It won't go away no matter what I do. At least now I know Jimmy is fine. I only wish I could look into his eyes and hug him one more time."

"I wish you could too, Barbara Ann. I wish I could bring him back to you. I can only say to somehow trust that he's near you even if you can't feel him as before. Maybe with time you may start to feel his presence more clearly, and you'll be able to hug him in spirit."

"I hope you're right. Thanks."

"Barbara Ann, please take care of yourself."

There is no time to deal with my own emotions. The door buzzer sounds, my client has arrived. She sits down, and her dead folks are suddenly there, all with so much to say.

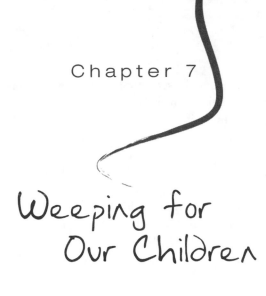

Chapter 7

Weeping for Our Children

I ONCE HEARD DR. PHIL McGRAW ON *Oprah* speaking to a woman who lost her daughter ten years before. She was still in a state of grief and despair. Dr. Phil presented this story, which touched me, as I understood the message so clearly. I will paraphrase it for you.

Everyday God gathers all of the young people, and gives them a lit candle to guide them into his garden. As they enter, his garden greets them with an array of beautiful trees, birds, soft waterfalls, and assorted fragrances of brightly colored flowers and most of all, serenity and comfort.

God would sit and admire all that played and enjoyed each other's company. This pleased him, yet he was aware and remained vigilant over one young child that would never enter into his garden. One day, he approached this beloved child and told him that he noticed that he chose never to come into the garden.

He then asked him, "Is it because he did not want to?"

The child looked up at God and said, "Oh, no, I would love to come into your garden."

God then said, "So, what is the problem?"

The child replied, "I cannot find my way because my mother's tears keep putting my candle out."

Séances involving children are my most intense, heart-wrenching sessions. Few parents ever get over the loss of a child. After finishing sessions with parents who have lost a child I often feel as though every part of a child in spirit is still part of the parent. It doesn't matter if the child is six or 26. They always remain your children.

🌀 🌀 🌀

There is no more devastating loss for a parent than the death of a child. Children are supposed to bury parents, not the other way around. It is not in the natural scheme of life. Our family sustained such a loss when we lost a son in May of 1992 after a long, painful illness as a result of AIDS.

It was the following August after David's death when his friend Christopher called to report an incredible session he had had with a psychic whom his psychiatrist had recommended. David, my son, had influenced my life to the extent that I had become open and accepting enough to be

intellectually curious concerning spiritualism.
I called Suzane and made an appointment for
a phone session at the beginning of September.

The analgesic shock of the loss had worn off
by that time and a deep sense of desolation, set
in as the full realization of the finality of David's
death had overcome me. During my session with
Suzane, I felt a real connection with David. She
seemed to catch the essence of his personality to a
tee. It was almost as if David and I were resuming
a conversation we had not finished earlier. She
relayed information to me that was amazing.
She had no way of having any knowledge of the
information she related. By the end of the session
the heaviness that had been surrounding my heart
seemed to have lightened. I knew that David was
well, safe, happy, no longer in pain, and back to
his old self again. How much more could a parent
want for her child? I know that his spirit lives on.

— Ruth

I AM IN AWE OF HOW PARENTS ARE ABLE TO MOVE ON AND PUT their lives back together. I am desolate for those who cannot. Finding your child again through a séance will bring healing. It is never enough. I can't bring the child back to you; I can only bring you to him, to learn that he is happy, out of pain and still loves you so much.

I have special help for this process when I'm dealing with children in a séance. A child in spirit named Matt. Matt walked through the door to the other side when he was twelve and died from leukemia. Even in our first session together, he was wise beyond his years on earth. Since our first session, and with the help of his mother, he has appointed himself to two jobs: helping other children in their transition and giving information about and from the children who have joined him to the parents left behind. Shortly before Matt's passing, he experienced seeing angels surrounded by light. He had been in the car driving down the road with his father when he looked up and saw his name up on a sign with an angel looking at him. "Look Dad!" he said, but his father saw no angels.

Three Days Before Death

Matt says these three days are very important. A long-term illness such as cancer seems to go into remission. An overnight miracle! A patient seems almost ready to go home. Well, they are, in a sense to the soul's true home, which is with God.

Do you know how many times I've been told, "She was out of pain, her old self again, I couldn't believe it. Then all of a sudden she died." Both children and the elderly seem to have a foreknowledge of their deaths, Matt says, within three days of death. It's during this three-day period when angels are seen, more often by children than by adults. Adults tend to see their loved ones who have already passed over, figures of wisdom, beings of light. Once again, what you need to see, you will. Children who believe in Jesus may see him, others may see angels, still others may see grandparents or other DPs who went before.

Growing Up Over There

Matt has frequently asked me to tell parents that children who passed over as children will grow up in the *spirit world* but not to worry, you'll recognize them! And yes, they'll wait for you.

Fear of Burial, Not Death

Matt has talked about the fears that dying children have—not of dying but of being buried. Matt was there to help bring over a little girl he had met briefly during his own final illness. Matt discussed in one session a deep fear the young girl had had prior to dying, of being buried forever in a box. Her mother, already grappling with her daughter's imminent death, believed neither in God nor heaven, nor any life after death. She had no words, no way to relieve her daughter's fear. The child had had several panic episodes and her mother was still terribly guilty. Matt was delighted to report that the little girl was doing well and was no longer afraid. She found out there was no box where she was. This particular fear that dying children have has been described to me, too, by other distraught parents.

Children as Helpers

Although Matt has been the most constant of the young DPs helping to bring over children, he isn't the only one. His story is one among many; others have done the same. During a private séance with Becky, her grandmother showed up in spirit and with her was a very young boy, five or six years old, and a young woman in her twenties. I knew immediately these were siblings and I had the impression that Becky was their sister.

Becky seemed overjoyed and deeply emotional. It was apparent that both of her siblings' deaths had left her with a deep pain and personal guilt. Scott, the young boy, said his passing was a quick one from an accident. It seemed to be important to him that Becky know it wasn't her fault.

The sister vibration became stronger. Her name was similar in sound to Becky's. I thought it was Beth but it turned out to be Betsy. Scott claimed he had been there to help bring over Betsy, who was his older sister. At the time of this session, Betsy had been in the *spirit world* for several years and Scott had been there double that time. It was obvious that Becky never really got over the loss of her younger brother and now there was Betsy's death to cope with, too. She and Betsy were only a year apart in age and had done everything together. She felt some consolation about Betsy being with Scott because Betsy, like herself, had never gotten over Scott's death. She was glad they were both all right and together.

Later Becky and I talked. She and her sister had been taking care of Scott when he fell out of his treehouse in the back yard. He died instantly and it was Becky who found him. Both sisters had always felt responsible. Now Becky also felt responsible for Betsy's death. She had insisted that Betsy travel with her to Italy one summer. Betsy really didn't want to go but went to please her sister. For her, the trip had ended abruptly. She was killed in a car crash while someone else was driving. This second death was devastating for the family and Becky was consumed with guilt; her parents got divorced.

The contact with both brother and sister helped to let Becky know that they were well and certainly didn't think anything had been her fault. This reassurance helped relieve the guilt and blame she had felt for years. She was so happy they were together. She felt especially warm inside to know Betsy had not died alone, that Scott was there to greet her and he was so proud to have helped her come over.

Children as Guides

Another little tidbit that Matt passed on to me is to be read only by those who believe in angels, spirit guides, or *other world* helpers. The rest of you should bypass this paragraph. He spoke to me about how children often become "joy guides" for those still living. What does this mean? If you believe you are helped by guardian angels or spirit guides, other than DP family members in life, then you will understand the concept.

"Joy guides" are sent to people who need special love and attention but who also desperately need laughter and to be reminded of how to play. Who better to do this than children? Children are often chosen and very much enjoy the job of joy guide.

Children on earth have experiences with the *spirit world* that most adults categorically deny.

EVAN HAD NO PROBLEM WITH ACKNOWLEDGING HIS NEAR-death experience. His problem was the limited minds of adults surrounding him.

I learned about Evan through a woman who was the executive director of research on Near-Death Experiences *(NDEs)* at Stanford University. She was working under Kenneth Ring who had in turn worked with Raymond Moody, another pioneer in the field of NDE study. Since this event occurred, several books and studies concerning children having *NDEs* have been written, but at the time of this experience there were few references.

Evan's near-death experience occurred when he was four years old. He almost drowned and his mother became deeply concerned about his behavior after the accident. Evan had been having difficulty adjusting to school before this happened and the experience of nearly drowning seemed to cause his problems to escalate. Evan's mother had never heard about *NDEs* or knew what one was until a friend of hers mentioned reading an article about current studies in this field at Stanford University. Evan's mother decided to write a letter to the director inquiring if an NDE could possibly have happened to Evan. She wrote describing how Evan had fallen into a pool and had been under water for ten minutes. Only days after the accident did she ask him why he was so quiet; what he told her about his experience was described in her letter:

> *"I was watching you and Pauli and another woman putting your hands on my body."*
> [His mother] *"Where were you?"*

> *"I was up on the roof and I was getting very*
> *tired so I started walking down a tunnel and*
> *there was a man standing there."*
> *"Who was the man, Evan?"*
> *Evan, in a matter-of-fact little voice replied,*
> *"Oh, it was God. It was very bright, Mommy,*
> *and all the people there were very nice and I*
> *wanted to stay and I put my hand out to God*
> *and God put his hand out to me and said, 'You*
> *need to go back to your mother. She needs you,'*
> *and then God took his hand away."*

When Evan returned to school after the summer he decided to share his experience during *Show and Tell*. The horrified teacher interrupted his story and sent him to the school psychiatrist. They both felt this was an example of an overactive imagination.

The director of the research project told me that Evan's school work and socialization had continued to deteriorate and that she was still in touch with Evan's mother. In frustration, Evan's mother had left the town where the NDE incident occurred, in the hope that starting a new life elsewhere might help get Evan redirected emotionally. I don't know how Evan has fared.

Another question I'm constantly asked is, "Is it possible my daughter could have seen my mother. She has been dead for years, but when I show my daughter her picture she says, 'I saw Grandma, mom.'"

My answer is absolutely, positively yes. Children see and hear many things adults have lost the ability to experience. They are naturally much more receptive (their right brain works on high voltage). They don't analyze what we call an "extraordinary experience," and they don't question the logic; they only enjoy what happens. The door for this receptivity remains generally open until the age of eleven or twelve. I've also learned that children as a rule don't have bad experiences with the *spirit world*, but rather with the negative reactions of a parent or some other authority figure regarding their *extraordinary* experiences.

A DEAR FRIEND AND CLIENT, NOW A *DP*, TOLD ME THE STORY of Davey, her grandson, and his ongoing encounters with her dead husband, his grandfather, who had died six years before Davey's birth. On several occasions, while Davey was in his bedroom, he could be heard talking to himself. This was not unusual for a three-and-a-half-year-old, except when asked whom he was talking to, Davey would reply, "My grandfather."

"What did he say?" his father asked, humoring him.

"Grandpa says he loves me and can't visit me too often but he would come see me again and he kisses me goodbye."

One day when Davey was three, his mother was having a very difficult time with him. He kept insisting he had spoken to his grandfather and he wanted "E-da, E-da." This went on all day. His mother gave him food, because that's what it sounded like he wanted, but that didn't work. He continued to cry, becoming more frustrated and angry. Later his father, Steven, came home. Davey's mother, herself completely frustrated, exclaimed, "I don't know what he's trying to tell me!"

Steven turned to Davey. "What is it you want Davey?"

"I want music, Daddy."

"That's not what he said to me!" Davey's mother said indignantly.

"Yes, E-da, E-da," Davey exclaimed.

"Oh my God," Steven replied, "My father's favorite opera that he played all the time was *Aida.*"

Steven put a tape of the opera on and Davey was very happy, now he could listen to "Grandpa's music."

The moral of this story: just because *you* can't see a DP doesn't mean your children can't. The importance of validating children's experiences is so important to me, I suppose, because I spend so much time validating myself and my work.

Matt helped with this also. I've known Linda, Matt's mother, for a few years now but all our sessions had been held over the phone. I had never met her until last summer. Interestingly, I've been feeling Matt's presence so strongly for so long, even though his mother was far away. Linda has decided to take on the mission of calling me not only for sessions in contacting her son, but to contact other people's children and beloved DPs as well. Matt seems to want his mother to do this; I know he helps.

My beloved son, Matt, died in my arms on March 5, 1991. I had never examined my faith in an afterlife or eternal life before. I felt it was possible to connect [with Matt] but in my own search to find a psychic to do this I had met one fraud and several psychics with mediocre abilities. So, I was apprehensive.

After my first conversation I was elated, bewildered and astonished all at the same time.

Suzane's descriptions of other people besides my son were very accurate.

On my last visit, and the first time meeting Suzane in person, I told a friend that I'd ask about her son Aaron. I sat down in Suzane's living room and the first thing she said, before I spoke, was, "I'm hearing two names, very loud and clear, Karen [the mother] and A-Aaron."

I gulped and said, "Keep talking."

I asked about other children and then played the tapes to their mothers. Suzane told me information about those children that I did not know but that was later confirmed by their moms.

I asked you [Suzane] about my friend Barbara's father. You said, "He went immediately, boom, and an Edith was involved." He shot himself at the age of 84 and hated Edith, whom he blamed for the break-up.

I asked about Diane. You said they had three children. I said, "No, they don't." They did have three. One died at birth.

I asked you if Matt was with any other child? You said, "Yes, a younger, smaller, frailer boy than Matt and that the young boy had died before him." Matt told Suzane that the young boy was very light complexioned, almost died twice, but stayed for his mom and was with a Martha. The boy was all of the above and when I called his mom she said he did almost die twice, and that his grandmother had died two months before and her name was Martha.

— Linda

THE BUZZER RANG. I LOOKED UP AND WALKING DOWN MY stairs was a woman, probably in her late fifties and dressed to kill. She had on her mink, wore jewelry galore and high heels, as though she was going to the Plaza Hotel, not to talk to a dead relative. She was followed by her husband who was equally well dressed, wearing what I call a "lawyer suit" (a three-piece suit) with a dapper tie. I liked him immediately, but with her, I sensed problems. I directed Herb and Sally to sit on the couch. She looked like she'd *already* seen a ghost and we hadn't even begun the session. I gave my what-to-expect scenario and then asked if they understood what I was about to do. Reluctantly, Sally nodded her head; Herb returned my smile. And so we began.

I had just started when I was barraged by members of both their families: his father, mother, and grandmother; her grandmother and a brother who had died at a young age before she was born.

In the midst of acknowledging all the relationships of their parents, I heard *loss of son,* followed by the name *David.* I then heard *Robert* and that spirit said that he helped bring David over. I couldn't quite place exactly who Robert was, but David was Herb and Sally's son. At first I thought Robert might be Sally's brother, because Sally had lost a younger brother 20 years ago, but this was a young man who had just recently passed. When I was blurting out all the names from the dead folks only Herb tried to help, and he seemed bewildered by who Robert was. He could only come up with a cousin on his father's side when Sally finally found her voice: "Herb, Robert is . . ." There was a short pause. "She means David's Robert."

"My God, you're right," he said. However, neither one explained it to me.

In spirit, Robert stepped back to let David talk. David shared his travels, his successes, his love for his family. He thanked them for being there and supporting him always.

As David spoke through me I was sure he had passed over either from cancer or AIDS. Both illnesses give me the same sensation; my whole body feels compressed. I decided to ask Sally, whose eye make-up was now running down her face, "Did David die from AIDS or cancer?"

"AIDS," she achingly answered. I sensed that Robert had died from the same dreadful illness. As David talked, he made me realize that he didn't live long after Robert's death; he couldn't handle the loss of his friend and lover, and had soon followed Robert into the *spirit world*.

David had believed that you are put into this world to do something important in your life, to leave your mark. He had traveled extensively working for VISTA (Volunteers In Service To America) and other organizations that helped others help themselves. Without any compensation, he had also given his time and energy to children's aid and causes.

David then wanted to let his parents know—especially his mother—that before he passed he made sure his brother Richard had gotten married. David had even introduced his brother to the person. "Mom, I want you to know I stayed around until Richard got married. He was really unhappy being single. I hoped you would approve."

Up until now there had been a lot of love, energy, and intimate sharing between David, Sally, and Herb. Abruptly, I felt a wall go up. Through me, David talked incessantly about how important this relationship was for Richard and how happy Richard was, but his parents were completely silent.

"Mother, Richard is finally content, happy sharing his life with someone who cares and will be good for him." Sally finally responded, "I don't know what David means about Richard's marriage."

"Well, I'm sorry, but this is what I keep hearing him say. Is Richard just living with this person, I offered. "I'll often sense that as a commitment, a marriage."

Sally tried to compose herself. "You see, Richard is . . . Richard is . . . living with a man."

The wall and resistance all made sense now. "Sally, don't you understand, in the eyes of David, Richard is married, committed to the person he loves. David felt the same way toward Robert."

All this seemed to affect Sally more than Herb. A painful task for parents to face society's taboos, to have two of three sons homosexual. Herb seemed to have come to terms with David's lifestyle, he was proud of his son's professional successes and personal commitment to helping others.

Now, he only wished that his son were still here, alive once more so he could hug and hold him again. David wasn't at all apologetic about his sexual orientation, his only worry was about his parents' grief and their attitude toward Richard.

I can only bring the living and the dead together; resolution is up to them. I don't know if Sally's acceptance of David's choice was real or feigned. David obviously believed she had supported him. His death as a result of

AIDS may have crushed her. Was she fearful and in denial about her second son? I don't know.

Some parents come to me desperate, some defensive, and I don't blame them. They've been hurt so much already, they don't want to be hurt anymore.

MR. D CALLED WANTING AN APPOINTMENT, BUT HE WAS VERY curt and brusque and announced he did not want to give me his name. He said he wanted to set up a phone session, and he didn't want me to know anything about him, such as who he was, his phone number, or who had recommended him (which I rarely ask anyway). Payment would be made in advance via a friend in New York. I wouldn't know where he was from.

I set up an appointment, seething, and then lost my temper. "I don't care if you don't tell me anything. I don't want to know anything about you anyway!"

I banged down the phone, angry at him and angry at myself for not being more firm with my professional policies. I ask for a phone number in case I need to reschedule, and I need a confirmation of time and date even if I don't know a client's name.

I did receive a check so I assumed *Mr. D* would call for his session. He did call at the appointed time, but politely asked if he could call an hour later because he wanted his wife to be on the other line. I was intrigued by his demeanor, it was so different from that of his first call.

He did agree to give me his name. I later learned he lived in Washington, D.C. I knew nothing more. I never heard from him again after his session. I remember the emotions but none of the details of that session. It wasn't until the writing of this book that I learned he had been recommended by Linda, the mother of my spirit helper Matt. She had asked several people to write of their experiences at their sessions and *Mr. D* was one who responded. He was the last person from whom I would have expected a testimonial letter, and yet when I read it, it brought me to tears.

The letter is, as I received it, not really a letter, but more of a transcript with commentary. I had taped the call and sent it to him. At the time he had responded to my information with only "yes" or "no." As a result, I never knew whether or not anything I had told him was accurate or had been of any help. His commentary in the letter gave me some of the background details and an affirmation moving in its strength and simplicity.

S: Who has a walking problem?

D: That's me. Also Jake, our late son, when he broke his leg. At the time, I was so surprised by that that I didn't connect it to me at all, although I remembered his broken leg. But I had a severe case of phlebitis that struck me—a healthy, exercising 39-year-old male—about six months before my conversation with you. I was in the hospital for a week and out of work for three more before it cleared up.

S: He is identifying himself to the person with the walking problem.

D: Of course, Jake identified with me (problems with legs his and mine), and until we repeated the tape, neither of us got the connection.

S: Roses, strong smell of roses.

D: My wife's grandmother long dead had a rose garden. She said it was a very vivid memory as a kid for her.

S: I'm hearing an M name.

D: My sister's name was Marilyn. She died at age 14 months from pneumonia in 1941, nine years before I was born, 50 years before Jake died.

S: Parents live somewhere else distant. Did you just visit them?

D: Jane's parents had just left a few days before, after a one-week visit for Jane's graduation from nursing school for her nurse practitioner degree.

S: Who lost a child?

D: Us.

S: Was this a long illness? I'm getting long-term.

D: Two of them, actually. Cystinosis since birth, then lymphoma.

S: I got a tremendous pain in my head.

D: Jake had headaches from a number of things -the two prime ones being radiation and chemotherapy effects, and his sensitive eyes from cystine crystals. In 1990, we had to stop one chemo, asparaginase, because he developed a noticeable clot in a vein atop his skull. It was a side effect of the medicine. It was not life-threatening, but it cut off blood flow in one vein and looked real bad, and we remember that he had bad headaches until the effects of the drug went out of his system. It was a rough month.

S: Was it an organic illness?

D: Yes.

S: There are two more children?

D: Yes.

S: A lot of things with his eyes. Were there problems there?

D: This was little known about Jake, but he had photophobia, or an acute sensitivity to light. He had had it from birth due to the build-up of cystine crystals. The older kids with cystinosis need corneal transplants because the crystals are so bad. A few really bad cases have gone blind. The crystals are why he always wore sunglasses outside, and he wore them sometimes even indoors in fluorescent light. He wasn't old enough to self-administer eye drops, which were being given through the NIH with some very good results, to help dissolve the cystine crystals. So the crystals were painful, especially as he got older, because it's a cumulative build-up. It's described by ophthalmologists as feeling sort of like sore, scratchy contact lenses. He suffered a lot with this, but seldom complained, maybe because he never knew how good eyes are supposed to feel.

S: He wants you to know he's seeing very well now.

D: This was a great comfort to us. It sounded like something he would say, to ease our minds. At this point in the tape, I have to honestly say we felt we had connected with our son. We were both dumbfounded, awed. I can't quite describe how we felt.

S: I wasn't only Mommy's boy, but also Daddy's boy.

D: On the mark, we thought.

S: He's says he's very artistic, a lot with his hands.

D: Jake loved to draw, he was starting to play piano. He did a lot of craftwork because he was too small for sports. At the end, his big thing was Legos. He made about 40 models in his last couple of months.

S: Did he lose his hair?

D: Yes.

S: He keeps telling me that his hair is back.

D: Comforting.

S: I'm hearing the name Peter or Patrick around him.

D: This totally blew us away. Peter was his closest cousin, a year older. Lives in Illinois. Saw him at least twice a year. Pat is an older cousin, early twenties, son of my brother, Will, in Alabama. Again, we see him about twice a year. Pat's a computer nerd; Jake liked him a lot and played Nintendo and other computer games with him.

S: This is not a shy child. Very rambunctious. Really out there. This is not a reclusive kid by any means.

D: That's Jake. Even with all of his illness, he was very rambunctious.

S: This child also knew he was going to passover, and you must have discussed it with him.

D: Yes.

S: He says it was discussed. He said Daddy talked to me about it but Mama couldn't. He said Mama couldn't handle it.

D: This is exactly what happened. I talked to him about it in November, out near the 7 West elevators, just before his transplant. He got cranky, stuck his fingers in his ears and said he didn't want to listen; later he said it scared him too much, gave him nightmares. But I knew that he knew there was a chance he wouldn't make it.

S: He was a bit of a jock, too. I don't know why, but he keeps showing me baseball cards.

D: They were one of his favorite things to collect, especially during the illness when he couldn't play much outside. In his room the nurses had a calendar up and every day, after his medical routine, they would tape up a new card. He had hundreds of cards and he told everyone to buy him a pack every day and bring it into the hospital.

S: Did you get a new car or something after he passed?

D: Yes.

S: He said he was glad that you got the new car, because he said the old car brought too many memories taking him back and forth to the hospital.

D: This was right on the mark. We would take the old clunker '78 Volvo in to the hospital often because it was easier to park and I'd often go to work from there. The Volvo was at the hospital the entire last month, I think. Since someone was with him 24 hours a day, we just left it there. My pastor and I used it to take all of his things home from the transplant room (about 15 bags worth of junk) when he got switched to the intensive care unit. And it was the car Jane and I and my brother drove home without him the night he died.

S: Daddy somehow managed to get money for it.

D: A stunning comment. The car was a rust bucket, a real eyesore when we bought it for 900 bucks. Three years later, I managed to get 500 for it from the insurance company when the service station botched up an oil change; the transmission blew and I filed a claim. It was one of my biggest success stories in terms of cars.

S: Daddy likes to do things with his hands. He's not great at it. We always have to hire other people to come in and redo what daddy does.

D: Jane laughed a long time at this. This has happened, more than once.

S: You are living in the same place. You almost thought about moving. He says you shouldn't because you really like it, and I am not the reason (to move).

D: We had both thought about moving, but as time passes one does realize that moving will not change things, so we really didn't consider it. But it was mentioned and thought of, more privately than openly, I think.

S: He has a whole thing about his hair. He must have worn caps or something.

D: Jake had at least a dozen caps. He seemed to have periods where he'd wear a hat all the time, others when he didn't bother. I think he might have worn them all the time if he could, but he'd get headaches from them. I think he kept a lot of his feelings within about his baldness.

S: He didn't have leukemia, did he?

D: No. But lymphoma and leukemia have the same treatment protocol for children. The types are very similar.

S: He says neither of you have let him go.

D: That's obvious, I guess.

S: Counseling together at all? Daddy was stubborn about it for a while, but it took Mama to talk him into it.

D: This is exactly how it happened. Jane got involved in this bereavement support group at the hospital, went to one session and had a rough time of it and ended up talking me into going to the last six. We went to our last counseling session the day after we talked to you, Suzane.

S: Somebody must have fished. Who likes to fish?

D: Jake always was begging me to take him fishing but we only went a couple of times. I wasn't much of a fisherman. The big moment for Jake was when he caught a huge bass in Maine with [other] fisherman on a big charter boat.

S: I'm not going to yell at you, but Daddy I tried to tell you.

D: This is poignant to me . . . It's as if he's saying he wanted to fish more often with me, just for the record.

S: He seems pretty diversified. He must have also liked computer stuff or whatever. You know I used my mind also. I learned some of that from my father.

D: I use computers at work and he liked to fiddle with them.

S: He says that I didn't think at first that it would be something that I would become interested in, but I did.

D: After he was diagnosed with cancer we got him an Apple computer from one of those "child's wish" charity foundations. He didn't want one. He wanted to go to Disney World again as his wish. But he ended up loving the computer and playing with it. In his transplant room at the hospital they hooked up a computer for him, but he was too sick to use it.

S: He kept feeling that both of you were pulling apart.

D: This happened both before his death and after. Parents tend to drift away from each other in times of grief or duress, mainly because they don't grieve or stress out at the same time. So, one day I'd be up, and she'd be down, then vice versa. In partners who have lost a kid, the divorce rate is really high. We cope with it; it gets easier as time passes.

S: One of you would yell and the other would go off.

D: That's exactly the way we handle turmoil, usually Jane will yell and I'll disappear, go read the paper, go outside, whatever. Or I'll yell and she'll take a nap.

S: There is a door for another child. I don't know if you are in the market or whatever not necessarily a biological child.

D: Since this conversation, we have adopted again.

S: He keeps telling me about another child. They won't be as good as me, but you'll keep them.

D: This is pure Jake. It sounds exactly like something impish he would say.

S: Where am I hearing the name Ronald?

D: Again, this came right out of the blue. Ronald is another cousin, the adopted son of my brother in Alabama. He's autistic, now 22 years old. Often when all the kids would be out rough-housing, Jake and Ronald would be left together in the living room or whatever. Ronald doesn't communicate much but he is a sort of benign presence, always sitting around mumbling or just sitting quietly playing with some toy or pencil.

S: He's now talking about the male with the G or J sound.

D: Suzane is finally getting his name, which is mistakenly sounded phonetically as "George" in the beginning of the tape.

S: Mommy is emotional. Daddy's that way too but he doesn't show it.

D: True.

S: He keeps showing me something about pencils.

D: At this moment, Jane says she was taking notes and looked down and realized that she had written Jake's full name.

S: Did the daughters share a bedroom?

D: Yes.

S: They each now have their own.

D: Yeah, at the time of this conversation, two months after he died, Jane took the girls to Michigan on spring vacation and I spent a week doing over the rooms, wallpaper, paint, etc.

S: The room has a better view.

D: He's referring to our front bedroom, where his sister is now. Jake had it when he was little, then shared it with his other sister, Lisa, for a while. The back room was dark, smaller.

S: You must have a room with a lot of windows.

D: Probably a reference to what we call "the big room," our third floor study/playroom with two large skylights and end windows. He spent many happy times there.

S: Did this boy have blue eyes? He says it was one of his better features.

D: Yes.

S: I will be real honest with you: I do not think he wanted to be out of his home.

D: Jake would drive us nuts in the sterile room because he'd keep yelling, "I want to go home; take me home" at the top of his lungs. It was a way of venting his anger, I think, against us, the doctors and nurses, and the disease in general. He didn't really mind his short hospitalization and his trips to NIH where he actually got a lot of attention. But toward the end, he really had cabin fever and was fighting off depression. It made us feel depressed and guilty.

S: This was his desire, and you were doing what you felt was best. He obviously sees the picture more clearly now.

D: This is all so poignant it's spooky. It's like he's saying he now knows what it all meant, why we had to do it, and he's half apologizing for being a little twerp sometimes.

S: He talks about an awful lot of running back and forth. A lot of crazy running back and forth.

D: Suzane has that right. Twice a week was a good week for us.

S: It seems, from what I'm getting, toward the end he couldn't run.

D: Twice. First, when he broke his leg in April 1990, before the relapse. And the long recovery, complete with physical therapy, and then after his relapse, in the sterile room where he couldn't even move around. That seemed to break his spirit, just like a wild horse's spirit is broken with its saddle.

S: When he couldn't run, then it was kind of hard. It was kind of like the last straw. He's saying, "When I couldn't run anymore, then I knew."

D: There's nothing I can say to add to that. It's the way we felt too, and we sensed he knew, too.

S: I told you not to take me to the place!

D: He said these exact words to us when he was alive! This is so real it's scary; it's like he is continuing a conversation, but from another dimension. He felt we had let him down, because we kept telling him he'd get better and he knew toward the end, in his gut, that he wasn't getting better.

S: Was he eleven?

D: He would have had his eleventh birthday a few months after we called you, Suzane. He was only nine when he died.

S: Did you recently go to where he was buried?

D: Jane had been to the cemetery the day we called you.

S: It was a place made special.

D: Yeah. We picked out a custom design for the stone. It has a rainbow [from sister Dawn] and a heart [from Lisa] carved on it, as well as a baseball bat and glove and ball. It's a nice piece of work by the monument guy. We plant flowers in season, nothing unique here—hundreds of others do it there—but it is a place made special.

S: He's now talking about trains.

D: He loved them; on his last big outing in October, we took our family and his best friend to the Edaville railroad and to a train museum in Middleboro, where they had a huge room full of them.

S: He ends with a young boy who came in and out of the hospital that helped him. He said they didn't have a lot of contact but it was pretty important and they are together. And the boy's name is sounded with M, short like Mack.

D: That would be Matt [Linda's son]. He passed over two months after Jake. They were in transplant together.

That's the end of the letter. Thank you, Mr. D.

IN SPIRIT, YOUR CHILDREN ARE STILL HUGGING YOU. THEY NEED you to know they are well now and that they still love you, so much. They don't need you to "make it better" anymore. They are better.

The grieving process is long and necessary. Making contact with your child in spirit will not end the grief, but it may ease some of the anguish and become the beginning of healing.

Chapter 8

Sudden Loss, Long Time Sorrow

JULIA, A CLIENT OF MINE, LOST HER SON to cancer. The hospital her son was in offered grief counseling for the parents. In our conversation, I asked her if she had heard about an organization that was created for parents who had lost children through illness. She responded hesitantly, "Yes, but it wasn't a positive experience." Surprised, I asked why. When she went to the meeting she had introduced herself, telling the group she had recently lost her son to cancer. An awkward silence fell upon the room. Then one of the members in a the group bluntly told her, "You're lucky, at least, you had the opportunity to say good-bye to him." She found anger, where compassion should have come forth. She didn't hurt enough. Therefore she didn't belong.

Suicide

The full pain for the living of losing someone from suicide is incomprehensible. What we don't realize is that the shock to those who have taken their own life is also very real. Death provides no escape for them. DPs who have committed suicide discover a hard-core truth; you cannot kill yourself. Your essence, your state of mind, and consciousness remain, with full knowledge of why you took your life in the first place. Suicide won't solve any of the problems, it only eliminates the body as place or means in which to work them out. And the concept of curtailing one's own life span "before the allotted time" is very real. There is a blueprint.

I've talked to many dead folks who consciously took their own lives, feeling the other world had to be easier. At the time they could no longer endure any more suffering—mentally or physically. They wanted to be out of pain and were willing to accept any consequence, including non-existence or eternal damnation, to achieve that goal. Other DPs have said that drug abuse also shortens a life span and goes against the blueprint. However the life span is altered, there can be much pain, both mental and physical, and then spiritual confusion for the soul who ends a life before the appointed time. And there is always pain for the living. As a result, each session in which a DP has taken his or her own life is emotional and deeply moving.

Jennifer was 18 when she took her own life. She was an exceptionally outgoing, strong, seemingly indestructible young lady. She loved animals, people, and life. Then she became involved with a young man and completely lost her identity and her strength. Her family distrusted the man, Larry, but Jennifer demanded their approval. Her family felt they had no recourse but to allow her to marry him. Soon they discovered Larry was involved with drugs and had been abusing Jennifer and destroying whatever sense of self she had left.

Her family, distraught to tears, tried everything to let Jennifer know how much they loved her and would do anything for her if she would let them. She refused the comfort and defended her life with Larry. Then one evening, unable to stand any more pain, Jennifer drove her car into a vacant garage, left the car running, and died from carbon monoxide poisoning.

The session with Jennifer's parents gave me much to think about. They were deeply religious Catholics, believing that suicide was inevitably punished by damnation in Hell. While trying to cope with Jennifer's loss, they also had the agony of questioning themselves, "Will our beautiful daughter be welcome in Heaven or go to Hell or worse?" Jennifer, clearly and articulately, in the witty manner of the "old" Jennifer declared, "No, there is no fire and brimstone, and God didn't punish me. I punished myself and, worse, I punished the ones I loved, my family." This is true for almost all the DPs I've talked to who have taken their own lives. Each of them experienced separate learning and aftermaths, but, as with Jennifer, the constant theme was feeling immeasurably responsible to those left behind.

Jennifer repeated throughout the session her regret for not having the strength to confront and deal with her pain and her shame for the suffering she caused her family. She hadn't realized, she said, that this was one mistake you can't undo.

Death of a body is the end of that body only. If you are unhappy and miserable while living, death will not make it all go away.

Eleanor, Jennifer's mother, asked her directly, "Was this your destiny, were you supposed to end your own life by suicide?"

"No. We don't have the right to take our own or anybody else's life," Jennifer responded. "I ended my life before the right time. These and other things are what I'm now learning and confronting in the spiritual realm. I can do this in nonphysical spiritual school or in another life-time." Jennifer added, "Mom, if you don't believe in another lifetime, that's okay too."

Dear Suzane,

You have given me the best Christmas present I could ever want, that is, knowing that Jennifer is doing just fine, and that she knows how much we love her.

Jennifer's personality came through so clearly. She loved to joke and she really lived her life to the fullest. She had received a lot of trophies during her horse riding years, and these were wonderful times for her and my family.

My mother had arthritis that crippled her body. She was stricken with this at around 30 years of age. My mother [Betty Lou] died in 1952 at the age of 32 years. I was nine years old at the time.

When Jennifer died, I prayed that my mother, and other loved ones, would be there to help her. I just did not know if my mother would know about her or who she was. The messages that came through from my mother were wonderful; I had often wondered over the years if she would have approved of my life and husband.

During the last couple of weeks of Jennifer's life she was sick. I saw her about two or three times a week. The last day at the doctor's she was very upset at me for being there. I told her I loved her and was concerned about her. As I was leaving town after work, I saw her on the road and waved at her. She waved back and that was the last time I saw her alive. Sometime that evening, May 14, she drove her car to a vacant garage six blocks from the house where she lived with Larry. We have every reason to believe Larry knew exactly what she was going to do, but failed to even look for her until 6 P.M. the next day.

Jennifer was such a tough person, it was so hard for me and my husband to understand how she became so weak. Jennifer was never afraid to try anything, yet she was afraid of what people thought about her.

I apologize for the length of this letter, but I wanted you to know the value of your gift and how this is the first time my husband and I were uplifted since Jennifer's death. We needed to know the answers to so many questions.

— Eleanor D.

Second Chance

In spite of her conflicting emotions at the time of death, Jennifer's transition was easy. It didn't matter that she had taken her own life, she nonetheless had a strong faith in God. A complete transition may happen in minutes, hours, days, weeks, or months. Other souls I've talked to who, like Jennifer, were unable to withstand physical or emotional pain prior to their death, may or may not have stayed in respite. We call that state of resting *bardo*. Bardo also encompasses reviewing what did or did not happen in earth life. Some will need more rest, some will go right to "what happens next." Again, it's a process unique to each individual.

Cause and effect are always in balance. Jennifer had to confront her actions. Her problems would not and did not go away. Her family has the comfort of knowing she is not burning in *Hell*, but they also understand she only punished herself and the ones who loved her. Only God will help heal Jennifer and those who are still in pain from her passing.

When I experienced the loss of Peter and Bobby in my earlier days, I had no way of knowing that theme would keep recurring, and because of what I went through then, I would be able to help other people who lost their loved ones to suicide. Intentioned or not. Sarah was one of my first.

Sarah called me crying so hard I had no idea who she was, who had recommended her, or what she was saying. I calmed her down, and she told me in wrenching gasps that her 17-year-old son had jumped off the top of their apartment building in front of her.

Sarah was calling me from a hospital, where her family had placed her, fearful she would take her own life. She was in no condition for me to deal with responsibly, so I managed to get the name of her daughter in between her bouts of hysterical tears. I called Sarah's daughter, explained who I was, and after some hesitation, she told me the details.

Sarah had collapsed after visiting the clinic where her son, Jay, had been treated for depression. She had just been told that a young pharmacist had given her son the wrong medication. It was a mistake, but had been a lethal one. It seems after taking the medication, Jay walked out of the clinic in seemingly satisfactory condition, but by the time he got home the medication had overwhelmed him.

He walked into the apartment toward his mother, then pulled back, and began to shake uncontrollably. Suddenly, he ran out of the apartment and darted up the stairs toward the roof at manic speed. Sarah ran after him, and as she reached the top breathlessly shouting his name, Jay jumped and fell to his death. Sarah stood frozen in horror.

Sarah was eventually discharged from the hospital, still in a fragile state of self-blame. She knew the reality that the fault lay in the medication, but a part of her mind kept repeating, "I should have been able to stop him." Sarah and I worked closely in sessions with Jay coming through to relieve her horror and guilt. Sarah was finally able to put her life back together and trained as a counselor for parents who have lost children to suicide.

The loss of someone by suicide is difficult no matter what the circumstances. Sarah's story has a connecting point for me, considering that Jay came through to assist her in moving on. I work in a circle of meanings and relationships that twine and *re-twine*. I helped Sarah; she helps others. Also, long after my friend, Bobby, had died and I was finally learning to let the DPs through fully, Peter (the friend who had committed suicide in New York) came to me and told me to be at peace, that I had had no share in Bobby's death.

One evening while leading a class I kept feeling the presence of a young man. This was unusual because he didn't "belong" to any of my students and DPs don't just show up without any reason.

Still feeling bewildered about this man's presence, I decided to check messages on my answering machine after class. There was a message from a client who had lost her father and another message from a longtime client named Susan. Susan's voice was anxious and I returned her call immediately. She said her brother (she didn't give his name) was missing, leaving no word where he had gone. This was very out of character for him and she wanted to know if I could get any information on his whereabouts.

"Please don't ask me to find out if he's dead!" I said. Adamant about this, I started telling her what I did feel about her brother.

I first picked up that there was difficulty in his chest; I felt tremendous pressure and it definitely had something to do with his heart. It felt physical, but it also felt as if his heart had been broken, having to do with a relationship. Susan confirmed this. Her brother had married on the rebound after being left by a woman he loved very deeply. I also sensed that wherever he was, it was somewhere near the border of several southwestern states and near water.

I then heard the name Andrew. Susan replied that Andrew had been her father's brother, her uncle. I said, "That explains why I am hearing, 'Brother is here.' Susan I know this is going to sound strange, but there's been a young man here all during class and he's now saying his name is Andrew. Do you think this is your uncle Andrew? He does keep repeating brother to me."

At this moment Susan's phone beeped, letting her know she had another call coming in. She asked me to hold on. The phone call was from her brother's friend: her brother had been found, dead. It appeared that he'd taken his own life. Susan came back on the line with me crying, "Oh my God, I didn't want to believe it, but it's been my brother who's been talking to you all along, his name is Andrew . . . Suzane, I'll call you later."

I was quite shaken. Andrew came through so strong and he'd only been dead for two days. And how could he have known Susan would contact me?

A few days later Susan called to let me know her brother had shot himself in the heart. It happened near a waterfall that bordered three southwestern states. Susan wanted to tell her mother that Andrew came through via me, but she felt her mother couldn't handle it. I would talk with Susan over the next two weeks. It would be a month before we would have a session.

Here are Susan's notes.

Sunday, August 6, 1987:

I saw my brother for what was to be the last time. He seemed remote, agitated. I couldn't quite place it, but he was not himself since my concern at the time involved job and career. I assumed

Andrew was also under stress due to work, his recent marriage, and an impending move to a new house.

August 7:

I visited Suzane to seek career guidance. As she went into an altered state, she suddenly jolted forward. "Your father's here," she said, "and he nearly knocked me off this chair."

She continued, "He's very upset. I'm getting something about Andrew. It sounds like Andrew is going to bailout. Wait, now others are joining— it's a chorus: Andrew is going to bailout. They're upset. You're going to have to help out, talk it over." I didn't understand the message entirely. I thought perhaps Andrew's marriage was a mistake and he'd ask for a divorce, or that he'd need a loan to avoid business trouble. But Suzane could not clarify for me. All she could convey was agitation and concern for the fact that Andrew planned "to bailout." I was puzzled. My job was safe, but Andrew's situation was puzzling. I decided to wait and see how I could be of help to him.

August 8:

As I'm lying on the acupuncture table during my lunch break, I'm unable to relax. The treatment normally puts me to sleep but not today. A voice in my head keeps saying: "Something's going to break." That night as I walk home from work, I hear the same voice, with the same message.

August 9:

Walking home from work, I sense a foreboding. The voice comes again: "Something is going to break."

That evening, a phone call comes from Andrew's wife of 16 months: "Andrew is missing. We haven't been able to locate him since August 8th. He disappeared around noon. His gun is missing. He left his money and credit cards on the table. This has been hell. Your mother doesn't know. I don't know if I can take another night of this!"

She told me that Andrew had been depressed because work was not going well. Ten days earlier they'd just bought a new house. And now he was missing. I was sick to my stomach. I began calling friends to ask them for advice. Then I called Suzane. I left a message on her machine: "Suzane, my brother is missing. Should we be concerned? I have a feeling he's with his ex-girlfriend in Denver. Can you help?"

The time was around 8:30 P.M. More calls: to close friends, to the police, to friends out of state, to my sister and her husband in Arizona, to Andrew's wife. It was now about 11:30 P.M. and I don't know where to turn. I'm wondering if Suzane is out of town. The phone rings. It's her.

"Who's Andrew?" she begins. "He's been here all night. I was giving a class and he was here. He's young and quite handsome."

"That must be my Uncle Andrew," I replied. "He was killed in action during World War II at a young age, 18, I think."

*She continued, "No, I don't think so, he's
with your father, your grandmother, too, they're
all there. I think he's just crossed the threshold.
He's been here all night." I'm about to protest
again when there's an incoming call. I ask Suzane
to hold a minute while I take the call. It's
Andrew's friend.*

"We've found him," he begins.

"Oh, thank God!" I reply. "He's okay?"

*"No, the police found him." He continues,
"He's not okay."*

*"But he will be?" I answer weakly. "No,
he's dead. He shot himself. Twice. Through
the heart."*

I return to Suzane. "Is Andrew still there?"

— Susan

A year later, Susan's mother had cancer surgery. A few
weeks after the surgery, Susan's mother told her that while
she was on the operating table Andrew came to her. "It
was so incredible, he put his arms around me and told me
he was never going to leave my side again."

Susan's mother continued, "I know this may be hard
for you to believe, you probably think your old mama is
senile, but I feel closer to Andrew now than I did the last
few years of his life. Each morning he comes and is there
while I'm having my coffee. I know now he's fine and God
didn't punish him."

Susan was deeply touched. Here she had been waiting
and waiting for the right time to tell her mom what
Andrew had revealed to her in our sessions, and all along
he'd been making visits to mom.

YOU MAY ALWAYS ASK, WHAT COULD I HAVE DONE TO PREVENT this? This is especially true with suicide. One of the things that I've also learned is that a lot of times, actually much more than one thinks, people take their own lives not because they can't deal with their mental, emotional, or physical state of pain, but because they don't want to put their families through "it" anymore. This is a very key component in these cases.

Murder

What happens when someone we love has their life stripped away at the hands of another, murdered? That is the theme of this next session. This particular crime is still under investigation so the names and circumstances have been changed more than usual to retain anonymity.

Several people had already arrived for class when Donna walked in. She looked distraught and disheveled. I took her aside to ask if she was all right when abruptly I sensed the presence of a tall man in spirit standing next to her. I felt strongly this man had just passed over. He looked to be in his forties and was clearly connected to Donna. I heard the name Paul and in the same breath I asked Donna who Paul was. She stood there in shock as she told me he was her sister's husband and he had just been murdered. I said, "He's here with you."

Paul insisted on proving to Donna that he was in fact present. Through me he described how he was starting to lose his hair but was nonetheless in good shape for a man of his age. He discussed his proficiency with numbers and that he was the prime caretaker of his two daughters, Sarah and Priscilla. Donna was speechless at how accurately this characterized him: he was vain about losing his hair and had been considered a top auditor with a *Fortune 500* company.

Paul continued to say that he had been met "over there" by his father and brother Anthony. Donna didn't think he had had a brother. (Later, I would learn that only Paul's wife, her sister Natalie, knew about the brother, so at the time, Donna thought this statement was wrong.) Paul continued, asking Donna to tell his family how much he loved them and regretted leaving Natalie with all the responsibility for their two children.

Donna was impressed that Paul was communicating his presence, and so soon after his death, but she didn't know if she should tell her sister. She was having her own struggle to believe in this, how could she expect her sister to believe?

Months later when I met Donna and Natalie together, I was told the tragic story. A friend of Natalie's, Jan, was staying with them because she was afraid of her often violent husband. All was well for a while. One evening, confident everything would be okay, Paul drove Jan home to pick up a change of clothes. Her husband had been stalking her and followed them into the driveway. He took out his gun and shot them both, killing them instantly. Paul and Jan were the only witnesses to their own deaths.

During our session, Paul, through me, told Natalie that he had found peace in his life right before making his transition. Natalie told me what he meant. She and Paul had had several rocky years and since the birth of their daughters,

Paul's life was beginning to turn around. Paul then told us he had passed over quickly, being met by his father and brother.

Brother? Natalie was stunned to hear mention of the brother. Paul's father had had a son out of wedlock, Anthony. It had always been hush-hush within the family. Paul hadn't even known; he found out about his half-brother only six months before his own death, when the brother was killed in an automobile accident. Only Paul himself could have given me this information, no one else knew, Natalie said.

Natalie asked if he felt pain when he died from the gun shot. Paul, said no, he felt no pain. (Many of those who have passed over from tragic circumstances attest that they may remember the experience but not the pain itself.) Paul also told Natalie via me that he would always be watching over her and their daughters. At that Natalie began to cry, yelling at Paul for having left her. She blamed herself for letting him take her friend home and wanted to know what could she have done to prevent his death? She was struggling to understand it all and asking, would he please stop saying it was his time!

Paul continued to say he loved her and missed her but was happy. He again urged her to let him go and trust that he would be near. Natalie then sighed quietly and said she was glad he was happy; she knew he had not found that happiness when alive. "But ask Paul," she directed, "Did he sense something was going to happen?" He had taken out an insurance policy on himself just six months before his death.

SHIRLEY WAS MY LAST CLIENT OF THE DAY. JUST AS SHE SAT down on the couch, I felt an impact in the back of my head and heard a loud *BANG*. Simultaneously, a large flower pot in the middle of the living room shattered so loudly that the woman and I jumped ten feet.

"Did you have a son that got shot in the back of the head?"

"Yes."

I had to clean all the water from the pot streaming into the middle of my living room. Trying to be calm so she would be calm, I just went about cleaning up the mess as though it were a common occurrence, which it was not. I've never had a DP announce his presence so dramatically. Flickering lights, yes; gunshots and splintering pots, no.

I finally finished and sat down to talk to this young man who most obviously wanted his mother to know he was there. I couldn't quite get the pronunciation of his name, only the first initial. With that entrance not much else was needed anyway.

Shirley's son made it known he had had contact with his mother in dreams and she was receiving the information correctly. He wanted her to know he had not been involved with what he called *the wrong kind of kids*, he was just there at the wrong time. He gave her the name of one of the kids who knew the facts of his death (she knew exactly who he was talking about), but he said it would be hard to prove anything since the individual kid was afraid for his life.

He proceeded to say he knew his mother would go to any means to have justice done and put away those who had killed her son. This wouldn't be easy, but he knew there would be no way his mother would stop until she saw the young men behind bars.

Shirley confirmed that she had received a lot of information from him through her dreams, but needed more clarity. What I was telling her in the séance matched what she knew about the killing and the name of one of the murderers.

She came back to me for a period of a year to see if there was any updated information. Shirley knew there would be justice in the eyes of God but she wanted it on this plane, too. So far this hasn't happened, but she feels it is her destiny and that God and her son will guide her. The courts, however, are not going to use her dreams and my talking to her dead son as evidence! My end of this was done.

IN THE FINAL PAGES OF A MYSTERY THRILLER I READ SOME years ago, there was a detective that was good at solving crimes, but not the relationships within his own life, especially with family members. As the story is coming to conclusion, a murder victim keeps showing up in his dreams to bring comfort to the detective for not being able to protect her.

The detective felt that the murder victim had come to say goodbye. He was glad because he had never had the chance to tell the victim how much she had meant to him. He felt her appearance gave him a chance to set her free, not in despair, but with love. He had truly loved her and when he woke, he wept for her and everyone he had ever loved. He wept for all those whom he had not the opportunity to say goodbye to in person before they had crossed over. What he came to realize was that what is done is done. When someone we know crosses over, their work is usually done while ours is yet to be finished.

The theme that echoes past the last page is that the murder victim did not have to come back. Her "life" was over. But she did come back, because she did not agree that her "work" was over. Perhaps a *spiritual hug* was all the detective could handle at the moment, but she gave him that much, and opened his eyes to the possibility of a richer life.

Chapter 9

When Decisions Must Be Made

Living Will

JENNIFER AND ANDREW HAVE NOT BEEN THE only DPs who have talked about death from suicide, for there are circumstances that to some are considered suicide or murder which might be viewed a bit differently by others. This came up in a session with the question of a living will. Mrs. June Simons had been diagnosed with Alzheimer's disease in June of 1989. She lived with her husband who had gone through heart surgery six months prior to her diagnosis. They had three children, two of whom had families of their own and all of whom lived in different states.

Just before Bill's surgery, he told his wife he wanted to have a living will done, in case something went wrong with the operation. He was adamant about not wanting to burden June and his children emotionally and financially. Reluctantly, June agreed. Her religious background left her believing euthanasia was out of the question, a sin in the eyes of God. However, she also knew Bill was much too dignified and proud to have his family see him be kept alive by a machine, and she also felt that with all her children so far away, she couldn't handle the situation emotionally or logistically.

Bill's surgery was successful and the family celebrated— only to later learn of June's Alzheimer's symptoms. Again, they talked about preparing living wills. Bill still felt convinced of the practicality of preparing such a document, while June remained deeply conflicted.

June began to deteriorate rapidly, going in and out of lucidness. Bill, still recovering from his surgery, was concerned that he was not well enough to care for and watch over June. All of this was beginning to place a lot of strain on him and the children.

It was during this period that I received a call from their oldest son, Bill Jr. He had been a client of mine for a few years and he visited me every year when he came to New York. He and his wife had two sessions with me right after her father's death. This had brought solace to her, and Bill Jr. now thought maybe one of the DPs from his own family might have some insight on his parents' dilemma.

Bill Jr. had come to New York and visited me in the autumn of 1990, a year before his father's surgery. At that session his paternal grandmother, who had become a DP twelve years earlier, showed up, expressing concern about her son's heart problems, which at that time didn't exist or at least no one knew about yet. Bill Jr. remembered this session when his father's condition became apparent. He was, in away, prepared for it. After all, his father's mother had spoken to him about it and she loved her son dearly.

In the current dilemma about June's illness, neither Bill Jr.'s father or the rest of the family knew what June really wanted for herself in terms of life support, if any. They knew what she considered a "sin" and they knew what she had agreed to, reluctantly, for her husband.

Both Bill Jr.'s maternal uncle and maternal grandfather had died from complications of Alzheimer's disease. His uncle had died within a year of being diagnosed, but his grandfather had lingered on for ten years. The grandfather had lived with June and Bill, so Bill Jr. had watched his grandfather deteriorate; the last two years had been exceptionally bad. His grandfather had been physically well most of the time and June had cared for him at home. His actual death happened quickly so the family wasn't faced with the dilemma of considering life support.

These memories ran through Bill Jr.'s mind, along with great emotional conflict. He didn't feel he could go through this again with his mother. Meanwhile, his father wanted the living will. Nonetheless, his mother, in sound mind, had to want it, and sign it. You cannot do a living will for someone else.

Bill Jr. wondered what his grandfather, having experienced Alzheimer's, might say, or whether there was anybody else "upstairs" who could shed some light on such a difficult decision. This prompted him to call me.

During the séance his maternal grandmother showed up, accompanied by his maternal grandfather, the one who had died from Alzheimer's. Bill Jr. was elated, for here were exactly the folks he had been wanting to talk to. His grandfather had been deeply religious, priding himself on his knowledge of the Bible. He had taught Sunday school when Bill Jr. was growing up, and now he said that between his religious knowledge and having had Alzheimer's himself maybe he could advise his grandson on the situation. Bill Jr. knew that much of his mother's religious conflict stemmed from her father's teachings, which in various situations created much distress for Bill Jr.'s own father and the rest of the family. However, Bill's grandfather had learned a great deal of tolerance since he had crossed into the cosmic realm.

Later, Bill Jr. and I discussed what his grandfather had said. These are the notes I jotted down afterward.

> The purpose of the soul is to continue to learn and grow. There can be learning in a physical body that cannot be learned here, in the spiritual realm. It is for this reason that a body is so important. However, if the body cannot continue to be a vehicle for the soul to grow, then the soul will begin to pull away and leave. If the soul has completed all it has to learn, and the body can no longer be the vehicle for this learning, "pulling the plug," so to speak, is not considered suicide.
>
> However, the soul, with full knowledge, must still carefully make this decision. It is not a decision to take lightly. As for me, my soul had been preparing to leave, but my body was in good working order, so I stayed longer than I probably should have. In this circumstance

I have to say that if the body is not serving the soul's purpose, it might be better to move on. But let me repeat this, only the soul can make this decision and that decision must be considered very, very carefully.

If others are involved, either because the individual is in no condition to decide, or because the ill person has asked for their help, all must agree. It is important that the entire family agree without feelings of guilt and trust that they, in aid of the soul, with God's guidance, and to the best of their own knowledge have made the right decision. With this, keep in mind, God does step in and put all the soul's learning into balance. For you, my grandson, the difficult task will be, however, to act as the catalyst to discuss this with the family. Do it now, while your mother is of sound mind and able to decide her fate and that of the family. Your father is much too close and vulnerable to make this decision on his own. Be strong. My love is with you and your mother.

In the end, Bill and his family did not have to face the decisions of whether or not to begin life support and to what degree, and then whether or, not to terminate it. Within a short time after our session his mother went into a coma, dying a month later. Bill's dad is still alive.

Life Support

Most of my sessions regarding suicides are similar to Jennifer's. But not long after that session I encountered a painfully difficult private session where a husband had to make a decision about terminating life support for his wife who could not live without it. This is one session I shall never forget.

It's not often that I become emotional in my séances and when it happens it's usually in a single, one-on-one session. It's imperative that I work with a clear head so that I remain simply the medium—the channel for information to come through, although the channel is also human.

Howard walked in the door, dressed impeccably, and carrying a briefcase. I immediately liked him. He sat down. I asked him, did he know what I did? He replied, "I have no idea, my friend just said I should see you. "Within seconds, standing next to him in spirit was a young woman. At first it felt like she might have been a sister, but I sensed "there was a baby with her. I then heard the initial C and another name that sounded like Alice or Alison.

Howard began nervously wiping the tears from his eyes. Alison was his older daughter. He then told me the spirit was his wife, Carolyn. I asked if he knew who the baby was. "My baby, a baby girl."

His wife kept saying, "the baby died immediately but I went into a coma." She continued by adamantly stating that he had done the right thing, for she was no longer there. This seemed to be very important information, because she repeated it over and over again, "You did the right thing. Please don't blame yourself or feel guilty; I thank you for doing what you did. It was what I would have asked of you." She then talked about a legal case he had been working on. How it came to pass and how he had won.

Carolyn continued to let him know she knew she was his only love and how they grew up together. "Our daughter,

Alison, looks just like me and I visit her often. I know it was difficult for you to remarry, but it was the right thing, for you were meant to have other children. You lost one daughter only to get another."

The love that flowed through me from this woman to Howard was one of the most deep-seated loves I've ever encountered, and so strong that I had to keep myself from being totally pulled in emotionally. After all, I was in the middle. I felt for this man. This was one relationship that will go on in another lifetime I'm sure.

I still hadn't made sense of what she was saying, because I kept hearing her say she had been in a coma at the time of her death. The other information she felt important was that somehow her body was poisoned, which caused her to go into a coma. Then there was the question of the baby. Later it would all make sense.

To break up the intensity, I asked Howard if he had any questions. Hardly able to speak, he could only say how much he missed her. A few moments of silence went by, he then told me what had happened. It gave him much relief to talk about it.

Carolyn gave birth to a baby girl. Apparently, something went wrong, she was supposed to have had a Caesarean birth but went through regular labor. The placenta was not completely expelled and complications proved toxic to her body. Within 24 hours the baby died, and shortly thereafter Carolyn had lapsed into a coma. Seven days into the coma she was put on a support system. It was at this time that Howard knew without question Carolyn was gone. He didn't know how he knew, he just knew. The internal conflict was horrific.

Carolyn remained on support for six months. Howard needed to know what his options were, what the prognosis might be of any recovery. He contacted a known specialist on comas at a major hospital medical center. The doctor requested a photograph of Carolyn before he went to see her. Howard thought this odd, but didn't say anything.

The doctor then went to see Carolyn. Coming out of her room, he told Howard, "I've seen this before. It's difficult for me to explain, it's not a religious thing, but she's not there. That's all I can say."

Howard had felt sure Carolyn had "left" the day she was put on life support. Now, finally, he knew without a doubt what to do and his decision was made; two days later he terminated support for his beloved wife. Somehow he had to put the pieces of his life together and there was Alison, their three-year-old daughter, to consider. Nothing would be the same. He hoped that Carolyn would forgive him and that he was doing the right thing. Carolyn as a DP answered his prayers, "Yes, you did, I was not there."

I remembered Bill's grandfather as Carolyn echoed his idea. To the DPs, euthanasia is not considered murder or suicide if the soul can no longer learn, because the body is incapable of continuing as intended. In essence, the soul's learning in this particular lifetime is finished.

This is still a decision requiring deep thought and contemplation. That contemplation should involve the person whose life may be ending and then those loved ones left here.

It is clear, though, that this situation is unlike conscious suicide, where discontinuing the physical journey intentionally leaves those behind devastated and interrupts the soul's blueprint.

There seems to be a firm line of thought that each person's path and transition is individual to each soul and to each soul's purpose. Additionally, we are given free will. As with everything we consciously decide, we must take responsibility. For that reason alone, we need to make our choices as carefully and conscientiously as possible.

THESE LAST THREE CHAPTERS HAVE EMPHASIZED A POINT THAT stands strong with me. Each of us needs to say whatever we need to say and to whomever we need to say it to *now*, because in a heartbeat our life and those around us can change. You'll ultimately be very glad you did.

I also, quite often in my seminars, have been known to ask for a count of hands of people that don't want to be left on *life support* when futile, and who have very definite ideas of how and what should be done with their physical bodies after death (i.e. cremated, etc.). To those "hands up" people I say, "That's fine except for one problem. You will not obviously be *disposing* your vehicle, so therefore it is important, crucially important, that you designate your desires in the most legal fashion you can, *while you can*.

It is extremely important that you share your particular desires with your family because I had one family that the son literally got arrested three times for breaking in his sister's house trying to steal his mother's ashes to fulfill her wishes of their disposal. The whole process between brother and sister ended up quite nasty and went on for three years.

Wills need to be done now, not tomorrow, if you know you have specifics to be honored. I believe every adult needs to have a will so that in the case of sudden death, those left behind are less hard-shipped by things being *unclear*. Having a will or not having a will has nothing to do on your life expectancy. It has nothing to do with whether you are going to *stay* longer or not. It is not a jinx. I wish I could tell you the number of people I have seen in sessions that have had tremendous struggles in many forms around the DPs that crossed with no clear instructions of what they wanted done. You have read some of the stories in these past pages.

Just for a moment let's think about the aftermath of the World Trade Center in New York, and other events of the September 11, 2001 tragedy. Below is an example how devastating it can be for families faced with the unexpected and the importance of taking care of things *now*.

When those towers came down and all those lives were lost, the big thing was that they did not have any physical remains to relate to, just the "place." Cemeteries are created for the living because we need a physical place to go to relate. This is why when there are no physical remains, we see things like people going to the location where the person was last, taking mementos, and doing ceremonies. This represents that physical presence when there is none. We, the living, need to have something to honor in terms of the physical relationship to the person lost.

No one will question that loss by any sudden death, whether it be accident, suicide, war, or murder will leave deep-seated pain for those loved ones left. Scars of unspoken words, of guilt for what was never said and no longer any chance to say. This is especially true when a passing is unexpected and abrupt. There seems to remain that feeling of emptiness in and around your heart that aches for connection just one more time.

Because both the horror and the loneliness felt by the bereaved are so great, when contact with a loved one in spirit is made, it offers much needed solace, comfort, and resolution. Making contact with your dear ones will give you an opportunity to say what was never said, to weep without shame for what you have lost, and to grow slowly in peace for what you now have found.

Chapter 10

Questions and Answers

I DO SPEND A LOT OF TIME ANSWERING questions, whether they are asked sarcastically or honestly. What happens when we die? Are we met by loved ones? Is there a Heaven or a Hell?

My answers are not "mine"—they come from the DPs. And with the dead folks, as with the living, there are no set rules or absolutes. Each answer is individual to each soul, *living or dead*. The repercussions, consequences or influences from one person's life-death process may be totally different from another's. The way in which we pass into the other world, even if under the same circumstances or illness, will be completely different for each of us.

Below you will find some of the most frequent questions I am asked and my response.

What Does Happen When We Die?

In order for anybody to understand a little about the death process, one must first believe—or at least be able to suspend disbelief—that you are more than your body, that you can exist with or without your body. It doesn't matter whether you define this as your spirit, soul, or just "you" continuing. Physicists know energy does not die, that it only changes in form. "Dust to dust" can be extended to "spirit to spirit."

This is what happens: your body dies, you go on. Period. Believing that you go on, even if you don't know where, will help you in accepting and comprehending the death process. These answers I have received from the dead folks. Many a dead person has expounded on what has happened to them during their death processes, although it doesn't seem to hold the same importance to them as it does for the living relatives connected to them. The living apparently have a need to know if the dead are all right and what happened to them at the time of their death. For instance, are they still in pain or shock if they died a tragic death? The DPs have shared what happens during death and I describe the factors that influenced their death transitions. I have been given plenty of philosophy from the dead folks. One example is particularly appropriate: Dr. Leonard Grossman.

Dr. Grossman's daughter Ilene came to see me within a year of her father's death. She came hoping she could contact her father through me, primarily because she feared what might have happened to her father after his death. Her father had been a staunch atheist and that worried her. He was a psychiatrist with a strong interest in physics and astronomy. Dr. Grossman had lost most of his family from the Holocaust during World War II, and he was bitter. Science offered no proof of God, but if there were a God, he would argue, how could that God allow such an annihilation to occur. Death became his nemesis in life, and his beliefs and conflicts remained until his own death.

Dr. Grossman came through in the first session, and then, to Ilene's shock, her father's partner in psychiatry, Dr. Fields, now also a DP, decided to show up for the session as well. Dr. Fields had had no children and Ilene held a special place in his heart. Ilene enjoyed the session tremendously. She said, "It was like old times—Daddy and Dr. F. bantering back and forth, discussing philosophy and ideas."

Below is a distillation of Dr. Grossman's theories, repeated in several sessions, as close as possible to his own words, as best Ilene remembered them.

> *There are two important factors influencing us in our death transitions. The first factor is the circumstance of our death. Illness, accident* [Dr. Grossman had been killed instantly from a head-on collision with a truck], *war, or natural causes will all have individually specific effects and influences on what happens at the immediate time of our death. The second and more important consideration is: Our beliefs, faith, thought processes,*

and state of mind immediately prior to and at the time of death. Any of these may not necessarily affect the death process itself but will influence the soul's consciousness at the time of death. If we're in a state of extreme emotionalism, that is, fear from an accident, emotions felt after taking another's life, or the trauma endured from dying in war, those emotions or states of mind will travel with us through our death transition. No physical pain will be felt, but there will be variables in the immediate outcome. If you believe in some form of life after death, however defined, your transition will move quickly, as if in a dream state, into the light. The way you died might have been traumatic but your transition will be filled with love and guidance. However, the expectation of nothingness, or fear of that nothingness, fear of the unknown, or fear of punishment—whatever terrifies you— may keep you in a state of semi-awareness until you are ready to see the light. This is in essence what happened to me at the time of my death.

I believed death was the end, this is all there was and it's over. At the time of my death I went into a state . . . called bardo or respite. [Many DPs besides Dr. Grossman have described this.] In this plane of consciousness we may rest from the stress of physical life; we may review, judge, or understand the learning of our life, and we may even have conversations with masters about our souls' processes. The loved ones who helped me over, and the masters, told me I stayed in this state of being longer than I needed to.

*In life, everything had to be proven to me.
Proof had to precede acceptance. This demand
followed me into death. Eventually, after staying
in this state of respite, at some point, I realized I
wasn't dead. At that moment I became cognizant
that I was being cared for and looked after by
loved ones and family: my mother, grandmothers
and grandfathers from both sides, and my brother
who had died young. What a reunion! And
Dr. Fields was there, impatient to discuss our
latest experiment.*

As he and Dr. Fields bantered back and forth, Dr. Grossman reported that scientific laws held true. Everything in the universe is the effect of cause and every cause produces an effect-aptly stated in the Bible: reaping follows sowing. Energy changes form but doesn't die and that which is our essence, our soul, goes on; we don't die.

Dr. Grossman's personal beliefs played an important role in his state of consciousness during and after his transition. Our belief systems are very powerful. It takes a dramatic or devastating circumstance to change most people's opinions or firm beliefs about anything, but with regard to death, it takes a volcanic eruption. Or their own death.

This doesn't imply, however, that all those who believe death is the end will go through Dr. Grossman's process. What he experienced was his own cause and effect. Dr. Grossman stayed in his state of "unaware" existence or consciousness until he was ready to see the light. There's no pun intended with that statement.

If Heaven Isn't Above and Hell Isn't Below Us, Where Are the DPs When They're Contacting Us?

It's not so much the case of where we "go" as it is the state of consciousness we ascend to. Essentially the non-physical dimension is part of, and parallel with, the physical universe. There is no "in here/out there." These apparent differences are our perceptions only. Actually, we're all connected. (Sorry, AT&T.) Physics might better explain this time-space-continuum, and, in fact, there are some fairly mind-blowing, but accepted definitions of contiguous realities.

But as I understand it, we have two places that we share with God, one where we wear clothes (our bodies) and the other (when we become a DP) where we take them off.

Once we shed our bodies there is a different frequency or vibration to that energy level. This concept may be likened to the speed of sound or light. Vibrations or pitch produce different sound waves. The higher the pitch or sound wave the less it can be heard by the human ear, or at least most human ears, although we know other animals (e.g., dolphins) can hear higher pitched frequencies. Our bodies are made of dense materials (matter) that result in a lower vibration or less finely tuned frequency. Therefore, when we shed our bodies or when we are in an altered state of consciousness, the higher or more finely tuned the vibration, frequency, or energy level. This is the frequency the DPs are tuned into, and so in order for communication with them to take place we need to fine-tune our antennae.

The messages come in high and fast. Messages from the other realm go by ultra-fast, so fast we often miss or aren't aware of the experience. We don't realize that information is transmitted from our higher selves, or, for that matter, from the DPs. We can train ourselves to reach this level of antenna capability and enhance our sensitivity to what is happening. For most of us, this takes time and practice (for example, doing the exercises in the book) and making our minds truly open to more wonders than are dreamed of in our philosophies or beliefs.

Is There a Scientific Correlation?

Yes and no. Hard science discourse today sounds a lot like theories of Plato or Spinoza or the "nothing-is-real/all-is-change" concept in Buddhism: Mainstream physics is giving us a lot of room to make speculations that scientists would never have considered before.

Quantum physics posits a universe where everything is "happening" at once, but only perceive to the limit of the observer. Most human perception is, literally, the here and now—within space and time. Extremely complex computer systems are perceiving and making measurements far beyond the human capability. The "many worlds" theory adds that "everything" is happening all at once everywhere, with "everywhere" comprised of parallel universes and many dimensions. The multi-dimensionality is the core point.

It is now a given in quantum physics that the experienced nature of the observed is at least partially a function of the observer's interaction with it. As long as it is unobserved by us or unmeasured by a device, anything and everything remains only a probability. We also now know that the physical universe is composed of material energy fields in constant motion and vibration. What we call "solid" matter is really temporarily trapped energy, and within that solid entity is its "now" plus all of its probabilities, the potentiality of what it can be at the next moment, plus what it already is but across the road in other dimensions. Certainly, nothing dies, it just changes.

Neuroscience explains that the brain is a complex set of resonators, able to decode a wide range of frequencies. But only a certain range is known or proven. Is it possible to widen the existing range? That's still being studied. Beyond the brain, are there information-carrying frequency bands or groups of bands beyond the known electromagnetic spectrum? This is also still being studied. None of the new science offers proof of the DP-connection possibility, but it certainly now allows the possibility of the DPs and our connection with them to be considered. The doors have been opened.

A cautionary note here: Science deals with the physical world and it would be sloppy thinking to extrapolate from the physical constructs of multi-dimensionality—breaking the time-space boundaries or the capabilities of the human brain directly to "mind-spirit stuff." As a medium I can see some correlation, but I'll wait. They're getting there.

You've Said We Don't Go to Heaven and We Don't Go to Hell. So Where Do We Go?

The way we live our lives and our belief systems about death and what happens to our soul or spirit after death will affect the level of awareness we ascend to after our death. Whether we understand where we are in the afterlife and why we are there. Dante's *La Divina Comedia,* which includes more than just *The Inferno,* posited a model of levels of purgatory, heaven and hell—categorized by the sins succumbed to or overcome. True, there are levels in the next world but you cannot take a guided tour.

Level One
Earth/Astral Place

Your body, soul, thoughts, emotions, memories, and etheric body are all entwined together in this level or astral body. You still haven't, however, become an official member of the DP Society because you are preparing to go either to Level Two or Three. Where you go, whether it be to Level Two or Three, is determined by your beliefs or constructs and how well you did in your earth life.

Level Two
Lower Astral Place

I strongly believe that this level is the place the Bible refers to as Hell. Here is the gangrenous blob of all evil and negative energy, souls who have taken wrong turns in life. Their acts can range from murder, greed, addiction, to simple denial of death. Here are literally lost souls, who find themselves tangled in a web of their own emotional disturbance, trapped in Level Two. This is most often the dimension where ghosts abide, refusing to be dead or not aware that they are dead. Your state of mind, acceptance or not, of the new reality is what may keep you there until you literally see the light. Some souls never leave. Souls may end up here temporarily for other reasons as well-due to suicide or having died from a deliberate drug or alcohol overdose. However, not all suicides, murderers, or willful deaths will end up here. Everyone's circumstance is different, creating completely different consequences.

No one judges you. I repeat: *No one judges you.* You are allowed to do that by yourself. The compilation of your individual thoughts, deeds, and actions is what put you in this state to begin with. On earth you have options. Here in Level Two, lack of a physical body prevents any emotional or drug-induced escape. You are stuck in what many may assume to be a living hell. Someone who viciously harms another person without any conscious regret or remorse could be a prime candidate for Level Two, staying trapped in the compulsive essence of this state or act.

How long does this last? Once again, you and I cannot know and cannot judge. There is always a bigger picture we cannot or are not allowed to see. Is there a sort of waiting room, a limbo, or a place for transients in Level Two? I don't know. I do know some leave, some stay. Level Two involves repercussions, and there is a very wide margin of repercussions or consequences between, for instance, a man or woman having an affair and someone causing physical or sexual harm to another. In both circumstances pain and mistrust occur, but, in all probability, there will be entirely different consequences. This is not a punishment; it's merely the law of Karma—cause and effect—at work.

Whatever the circumstance, the actions you have not resolved while living must still be worked out after death. And then you get to watch the reruns of what happened.

Level Three
Intermediate Astral Place

This is where most people go, bypassing Level Two, to become official DP members. We will pass into the spirit realm, whether or not we have experienced physical or emotional pain during the death transition. We go into the light and awaken. There we are met by our loved ones guiding and helping to bring us over.

Naturally, your state of consciousness and faith will always be a factor in making your process effortless and easy. Those still in shock from a tragic death or long term illness may stay resting or in bardo until they are ready to see the light. Others may end up here after a long time in level Two. You will look as you did when you died, except that your vibration will be of a finer material. Later on, after recovering, you will begin spiritual school.

Level Four
Higher Astral Place

This is a grand place. It's the heaven you've read about. You get to meet with the angels, expand your views, thoughts, and awareness. This is the realm of total love without jealousy. You may even get to shed some of the astral body for a while before you decide what you want to do next. For example, you may decide to go back to Earth in another body for further Earthly good times or for more lessons.

Level Five
Mental Place

This is the last grade to be discussed here. This is where most of creation takes place, which is passed down to Earth: inspired music, art, and great scientific inventions. Who passes it down? It is passed down by those who have developed artistic or scientific abilities over several lives. These inspirations will then be received by those on Earth who are able to tune into that energy level or vibration. This is also the last level in which you can decide if you want to return to give Earth another go-round.

For perspective, consider this: everything you've done remains in your current memory bank, which works just as efficiently through your death as it did in your life. If you are wondering what kind of punishment awaits you, even in Level Three, you already know: the memories don't go away and then in this new state you must watch the universal video of your life's actions and be aware of the effect your life had on you and the effect on those you left behind. That is the punishment; what is the reward? To find yourself safe, surrounded by love, understanding, and acceptance.

What Are Out of Body Experiences and Near-Death Experiences?

Out of Body Experiences (OBEs) and *Near-Death Experiences (NDEs)* are the closest analogy or experience to what happens at the time of death. By all reports, there is no longer any fear of death for most people after they have this experience.

OBEs happen quite naturally during sleep, daydreaming or during illnesses. They can also occur during shock, as the result of an accident or during an operation while under anesthesia. Generally during an OBE the person wakes up and he becomes conscious. He also becomes aware that he is seeing his body from a physical distance, that he is hovering or floating above the body or seeing the body from the other side of the room. How the person reacts will directly influence what happens next. For example, if he becomes fearful thinking, "My God I'm losing myself," then within seconds, he will probably feel himself being jerked back into his body as though someone pulled a parachute cord. There is usually no harm done, just the shock of being jolted. Thousands of people have had these experiences, some more often and with more awareness and memory than others.

The safest OBE is during sleep. We all leave our bodies during sleep. If we didn't we would go nuts. It is important to remember that we are, in true essence, a spirit—a non-physical spiritual being. We are not just a body; we exist with or without, one. Sleep frees us from the physical body, at least for a little while.

NDEs occur as a result of a dramatic, tragic, or catastrophic incident, such as fatal accidents, clinical death or near-death during surgery, or a tragedy from war. Both OBEs and NDEs have been the subject of considerable scientific study. There have been many books now written about OBEs and NDEs by those who have had these experiences. Noted pediatrician Melvin Morse has described his research into near-death experiences of children in the book *Closer to the Light,* with co-author Paul Perry. The phenomena have been extensively studied by the pioneers in NDE research, Dr. Raymond Moody and Dr. Kenneth Ring. Dr. Elisabeth Kübler-Ross, a psychiatrist whose work with the dying and bereaved is internationally renowned, has said that she has studied more than 20,000 NDEs. Their combined studies, many of which have appeared in popular books and articles, seem to conclude that people who have had these experiences are no longer afraid of death. Now that is true freedom!

These scientists, the pioneers before them, and the many who will continue the work, will help those who need to have confirmation before admitting their experiences are real, even if not totally understood. Such confirmation is truly healing for those who have had this happen to them but don't know how to handle it. Children who have had this experience are generally not frightened, but instead matter-of-fact about what happened. Adults seem to have a worse time of it.

The story of David is a vivid description of an NDE. His story, and he himself, have healed many. Bobby, David's brother, was that first boy I met when I moved to New York City. It was during the last Christmas, when Bobby and I were together, that I met David.

David was older than Bobby by four years. The brothers had been inseparable since their father's death when they were both young. David had come home from the army for the Christmas holiday. He was on his way to Vietnam. Later, within two months of returning to duty, he was hit by a grenade and lost both legs. Bobby never got over his brother's tragedy. I have always felt that this deeply affected his relationship with me and probably with others as well. But after that Christmas I would not see David again for five years.

During the time I was getting my degree in music and coming to terms with my DP connections, I attended countless lectures on paranormal phenomena and metaphysics. NDEs interested me because I had learned that those experiencing NDEs often have communication with their dead relatives. This was right up my alley. At one particular lecture there were two segments scheduled: one on research and the other with someone who had an actual NDE. During the first part of the lecture a man and woman discussed their NDE/OBE research. In their studies they had found similarities among the reports of people who had had these experiences: going through a tunnel, seeing a white light, and meeting deceased relatives. Personally, I would have preferred a livelier lecture, but I was aware that these scientific studies were important for the more linear or clinical types. I hoped the main speaker would be a little more exciting.

I didn't have to wait long. Without any formal introduction, this tornado in a wheelchair zoomed across the stage, a guy doing wheelies in his spruced-up wheelchair. He expected and received attention from everybody. This man didn't have to stand tall or stand at all.

His story was similar to others I had heard about NDEs. It had happened, he said, during the Vietnam War. He had been hit by a hand-grenade, and both legs had been shattered.

He began:

I wrote a letter to my brother two months before the accident, telling him about the dreams I had been having. Nightmares that would wake me up in a sweat of fear. Something was about to happen. I felt the walls inside me cave in, closing me in, I couldn't breathe. There were so many fears during the war, but somehow this one felt different. Now I would call it precognitive by nature or a premonition, but at the time I pushed it away, hoping it didn't mean anything, only my fears. This can't happen to me. I have a girl, a football scholarship, a future. I thought I had life made, no one, nothing, was going to take it away from me.

Everyone in the audience sat engrossed, trying to comprehend. I kept staring at him. Didn't I know him? I couldn't shake it. Where did I know this guy? He kept going.

That morning I woke up. I had been having nightmares for the past week. They were becoming as common as the sounds of the jungle. It was two months before Christmas and I thought, my God, how much I miss all that. Where I am seems like a dream, yet I know I'm here, not safe at home. Not protected. God, please don't fail me now. My face itched from not shaving for two weeks. I needed something to pass the time, and cover the smell of the fear inside so I decided to shave, clean up before going back into the dugout. I remember it was Thursday. The day still haunts me. I still hear the noise. It happened so fast, that I never had time to change my destiny. My buddy, Dan, and I were on the front lines, hiding in the dugout. We were given the signal; the enemy was near. Dan ran out first. I watched him running and saw a Vietnamese with a grenade in his hand. 'Dan, look out!' I ran to push him out of the way. That was the last thing I remembered. All sound stopped for a moment, and then the next thing I heard was the sound of a helicopter. I didn't feel anything. I was floating above my body as I saw it being lifted up into the helicopter. It was an odd sensation. I didn't feel any pain.

For a moment all went black. My head was spinning. I was in a daze when suddenly I saw Dan and two other guys in our battalion. Thank God, he's all right, alive, I thought. It made me feel safe, not alone. I knew Dan was near, we were both shielded in the 'copter and alive. The blackness came again. When I came to again, in what seemed like minutes, I watched as doctors and nurses were working on my body. I still felt no pain. Suddenly, I became aware my father was next to me. "Dad, is that you?" I thought. "You're not dead! My God, I miss you."

The speaker stopped momentarily to more clearly describe to us his perceptions at the time. He had been aware of what was happening and whom he was seeing, while still thinking, this can't be real, it must be a dream. He knew his father had died when he was 16.

I was slipping in and out of this state of awareness. Now with my father were army buddies. Dan was there. I remember them all, vivid in my consciousness. I remember feeling the love and comradeship between us.

For days I fell in and out of consciousness as if everything were a dream. Several days went by before I was aware I'd lost my legs. When I did realize it, I was numb. In shock, I thought to myself, my life is over.

I thought about Dan. At least he had been spared. The doctor came in, explaining what happened, and the surgery he had performed. I said, "I know. I saw you working on my legs." The doctor didn't reply. "Can I see my friends? Has my friend Dan been around? I know he's okay, I saw him." The doctor became silent, as if he were trying to avoid my questions. Finally, I confronted him. "Where's Dan, and the other guys from my battalion? I can't believe they haven't been to see me, unless I was sleeping." Still no reply. This time I yelled! "Why haven't they visited me?"

With a blank stare the doctor responded, 'Your friends are dead.'

"I don't believe you," I said to him. "You're lying. I saw them and they were fine; in no pain, healthy, alive."

I became hysterical to the point they had to tranquilize me. It would be years later before I would ever share this with anyone. I never mentioned I had seen my father, too.

The room was thick with emotions. I was deeply moved. Suddenly, I realized I *did* know this person—he was Bobby's brother, David.

I watched him speak, eloquently and without bitterness about his fate. After the details of his ordeal, he talked of his search to learn more about what he was convinced was the truth. Six or seven years ago, he said, he knew what he had experienced was real but unexplainable, mystical in nature. He couldn't even find a name for it. At that time, 1971, there wasn't the wealth of information now available on NDEs.

David now knew he had had an NDE. He also knew, he said, that *We don't die. I've already experienced what we know to be death. I died. I saw my father; he told me it was not yet my time. I always thought this happened for a reason. Today, I know the reason. When the accident happened I felt God had played a dirty trick on me. I don't expect those who can't understand to agree or believe me. If I had not had this experience, I would have been skeptical, too, but without the experience I also would not have helped or touched all the people I have.*

The audience wasn't prepared for what David did next. Suddenly, like a trained athlete, he dramatically twirled and spun around the room in his wheelchair, staging a performance that left everyone in amazement.

This is what I do when I lecture at colleges about drugs. I use a little theatrical melodrama to effectively hit these kids with, you're thinking it's cool to use drugs and destroy your mind, well, see how cool it is to really lose something, for instance your legs.

Spellbound, we watched David throw off his blanket, revealing to all his legs cut off at the middle of his thighs. He shouted, "This is what happens to your mind when you use drugs, it gets blown up!"

His courage brought the listeners close to tears. Also, his explanation helped everyone who had questions, whether personal or simply curious, about NDEs.

I wondered if David would remember me. Years had passed. I stood in line with people waiting to thank David and shake his hand. He noticed me immediately and smiled. It was at that moment I knew two things: he recognized me and we shared a common bond. We both understood the essence of us, and we knew about life going on, not ending. We have stayed in touch and David continues what he considers his calling, to share with the young and the old that you must value what you have.

Ghosts . . . What Are They?

Hollywood has made millions of dollars portraying ghosts who have extraordinary powers, and do great harm to the living. Oh, they can and do scare the pants off you, but they are only as powerful as the power you give them. They cannot harm you but will prey on your own fears if you let them. In reality they're simply lost, restless, and want to get your attention.

Ghosts are trapped souls. Ghost souls are dead folks who don't consider themselves dead, who won't or can't accept the fact that they no longer have a body. They are literally trapped between both worlds, that of the living and that of the dead. This is not the same as being in respite. Respite is for souls that are healing in a resting state after a traumatic death or death transition.

Some ghost souls can't get past certain emotional fixations. They have not moved out of the Earth/Astral realm or the emotional state that obsessed and still obsesses them. Unaware that they are trapped, they stay in this state of consciousness indefinitely. Another circumstance is that of a traumatic shock-inducing incident at the time of death.

In either case, the ghost soul will remain close to the place where the incident took place (a war zone for example) or near someone to whom he or she was emotionally attached prior to or at the time of death.

Because the ghosts or lost souls are pulled to the Earth realm by their own problems, it's not uncommon for people to see or sense them. This sensing, however, is very different than feeling the presence of a loved one who has made clear transition.

Because the ghost souls are bound to the Earth/Astral realm, it is only the living who can truly help them move on. Within a religious framework, shamans, exorcists, and priests deal with releasing the lost spirit/soul. Mediums, who do this work, call it "rescue mission work," but don't call me, I don't do this work. However, I can describe one instance in which I did agree to help.

A young couple had bought an old house on Long Island, New York. The house had been vacant for years, originally belonging to a pediatrician whose office was in one wing of the house. The doctor had been married with one child, a daughter. He was very content until his daughter, at 4 years of age, contracted a rare disease and died. The doctor felt anger, guilt, grief, and helplessness at not being able to save her. He never got over his only daughter's death. He made his wife's life miserable until she was forced to leave and then he devoted his life to his practice. In his will he instructed the executors of his estate that his ashes were to be buried in the fireplace next to those of his daughter.

The buyers didn't know the history of the house prior to their purchase. Shortly after moving in, the wife became pregnant. Two months before the birth of their baby daughter unexplainable phenomena started happening in the house, particularly in the nursery that had been pre-pared upstairs. The door to the nursery would lock and couldn't be opened, lights would go out, they would be replaced and immediately blowout again, and the room remained consistently cold no matter what they did to get it warm. The door, the lights and wiring, and the heating system and thermostat were all double-checked and were all fine. The mother-to-be became increasingly upset and frightened, and talked about the house being "haunted." Her husband was worried his wife was becoming unstable. The odd happenings had to be explainable rationally. Haunting? No way, hocus pocus and nonsense.

Not until one night when he had his own encounter with the ghost did he admit his wife had reason to be upset. He had just bought a beautiful crib and he worked patiently upstairs in the nursery assembling it. However, if he left the room, screws and parts of the crib would seemingly be moved, ending up in various parts of the house. At first, he thought it was his forgetfulness but after taking several trips in and out of the baby's room, he realized the same pieces of the crib were being moved, in particular the headboard. After a night's work and a still unassembled crib, he decided his wife might not be so wrong.

The next steps were to get someone else to believe in what he and his wife were experiencing, and then they had to find help. I don't think this is information you are going to find in the yellow pages. Through a close friend, I was recommended.

The husband called me, nervously saying, "You probably think I'm crazy, but there's a ghost in my house." I replied, "No. I don't think you are crazy, but I don't deal with ghosts, rather with dead folks who know they are dead."

He was in no condition to discuss finer points of this, so after listening to his disjointed story, I finally said, "Let me see what I can do." I then called Mrs. M, another medium. She has since become a DP Society member, but, at the time, rescue mission work was her specialty. She asked me to come along and I felt somewhat obligated and so agreed.

As a rule, it takes two people to do a rescue, the medium and the conductor. There are mediums who don't use conductors, but in these circumstances, it's safer to do so. In the actual process, the medium allows the trapped ghost soul to, use the medium's body to express itself. The conductor's job is to ask direct questions of the ghost through the medium, attempting to find out what happened that would prevent him or her from moving on.

After Mrs. M and I entered the house, it didn't take long for the doctor, our ghost, to come through. He practically met us at the door. He had become entangled in his Astral-emotional body, refusing to move away from the place where his little girl had died. In his state of consciousness, he was never going to leave the place, where the daughter he loved had lived. Mrs. M then went into a trance state to allow the doctor to express himself through her. I acted as the conductor who confronted the doctor. He readily shared his pain and anger. The loss of his daughter destroyed him, he had withered inside, not wanting to love again or go on after her death. He said he wasn't going to allow another little girl in *his* house.

I let him know that his beloved daughter was waiting for him on the other side of life and that if he could feel her presence and see the light behind her and then go into that light, she would be there. He was not cooperative. He held on to his pain and anger possessively. With a little help from God, I was able to persuade him to relax his focus on Earth and to go into the light. I could feel the presence of his daughter who was waiting for him and I told him so. She had now grown up; if we die young we grow up in *spirit world*. But he recognized her and we had opened the door for him to move on. The doctor is now happily a member of the Dead People's Society and the house is at peace.

Mind you, I've also known folks who aren't bothered by living with ghosts and feel safe with them around. I once visited a "haunted" radio station in Canada. A few people quit, but most just accepted "William's" presence. Some even liked having him around.

Here's the story of another ghost who had difficulty moving on. The American Civil War left many a restless soul and there have been many stories of strange happenings as a result. The following is an account based on a news article in *The Daily Progress,* Charlottesville, Virginia, November 13, 1986. The ghost in question had terrorized a family living in Fredericksburg, Virginia, for two weeks.

His method involved hurling a crucifix across a room, one particular room, making books fly off the shelves and making doors fly open so forcefully they would come off their hinges. The family had been told a crucifix would make the ghost leave; it only made him angrier. The children became frightened. The parents went to the local priest who gave them holy water to sprinkle around the room and told them to keep the rosary hung on the wall. The events continued. Another priest visited the house. The events still continued. Finally, they called upon a local medium. Upon entering the house she immediately sensed the room where all the phenomena had taken place. She then saw a young, confederate soldier, about 16 or 17 years old. He had light hair, was in uniform and wounded, with bandages on an arm and leg.

The young man had been killed in the war and had died near the house. Apparently looking for a place to hide, he went into the house. He was very confused and scared, and he intended to stay in the house. (Ghosts generally do stay in the house or area where they died unless their attachment was with a person; the ghost can and will follow the person.)

The medium talked to him, trying to get him to go into the light where he would be safe and no one could harm him. It didn't take long for the frightened young man to understand and leave, and the family themselves then understood that he had been frightened by all the things they were trying to do to get rid of him. This is another example of a ghost who had no evil intent but was just lost and afraid.

A natural question comes up here. If the *spirit world* is so enlightened, why can't the more enlightened spirits force someone to come over and fully accept the afterlife? Well, when was the last time you tried to make someone do something against his or her will? Yes, we have free will even without a body. Or, better put, our stubbornness keeps us from accepting our fate and moving on.

Now that you are completely confused or a little nervous, time for a little philosophy: don't worry; if you stay true to what you feel inside, by listening to yourself you'll travel along the right road with a few bumps but you'll get there. The system is not quite as complicated as it sounds.

If We're Really Rotten, Do We Come Back as Cockroaches?

No! Although there are those folks you are sure are in the category of cockroaches, that is not the program. Cockroaches have their own destiny; they don't have to be bothered with getting rid of human guilt!

Pets, Where Are They?

Hanging out in the same place as humans. Many a dead folk have shown up holding their beloved pet. A better question might be, do they go through the same evolvement or levels as humans? Yes and no.

Yes, they learn and grow as we do, but they are part of a group soul. Precisely, we stay in human form and they stay in the particular part of the animal kingdom they belong to: wolves, dogs, lions, cats. However, if they have become domesticated, then they will often come back (or reincarnate) with the human family member they are connected to. Since animals do not live as long as humans, they may have the option—if this is what the human they are connected with wants also—to come back in another animal body in their order, to be with the human they love. I have no idea how often this can happen or if the process is different for animals that are not domesticated. I don't know all of the rules.

After Mrs. B passed over, her beloved dog, Muffin, was left here and her daughter cared for the aging dog. Recently the dog went over to the DP world to join Mrs. B. Her daughter knew that her mother would want Muffin to be buried with her so she had the dog cremated and took the ashes to the cemetery. She didn't notify the cemetery authorities that she was burying the dog's remains.

When she arrived, she cried, "Look, look!" to her husband. At the foot of the graveside where Mrs. B was buried with her husband, a hole exactly the same size as the small cylinder of ashes had been dug. Muffin always lay at Mrs. B's feet and this newly dug hole was in exactly the same place relative to where Mrs. B's body was buried. The daughter's husband (who thinks his wife's family is a little weird) went around looking at all the other stones to see if someone else had a hole dug the same way. There were none. I guess Mr. and Mrs. B knew Muffin was joining them.

The Story of Max

A friend said she wanted me to meet a psychic friend of hers who talks to living and dead animals. She continued to explain that a Los Angeles-based psychic, Samantha, was going to be lecturing in New York City and wanted music for her program. My friend felt I would be perfect, in part because of my ability as a composer, but also because of Max, my dog, who had died three years prior to this meeting. She knew Max and I had been inseparable.

Part of the work Samantha and I were doing was reconnecting people with their pets after the animals died. In other words, if both animal companion and person wanted to be together, she would know when the animal would be coming back in another body. Contact with dogs in the other world was something I knew could and did happen. But having them come back in other bodies to be together again with their persons was quite another thing.

Samantha was still in Los Angeles so we had to work long distance. We agreed she would send me the animal sounds she wanted to incorporate into the music to use for her program. She had done a great deal of work with the San Diego Zoo and had recorded sounds from a great number of animals. As I listened to the animal sounds, I decided they were instruments from their own orchestra. I would orchestrate the same way as if they were accompanying any piano piece I had written. The part that was odd was that while working on the piece I would look around my empty home and realize that this was the first time in my life I didn't have at least one "beast" living with me; it felt strange and empty.

Close to deadline, Samantha and I still hadn't met and probably wouldn't be able to until the lecture. One hot night in May, one of those nights when everyone was out, a friend and I went for a walk with her dog. I was sitting down on a bench when, suddenly, this dog came out of nowhere and sat next to me. Absentmindedly, I started telling him how handsome he was and how he reminded me of Max. My friend and I finally realized this dog wasn't moving and had been sitting next to me for close to an hour. Where was the owner? I asked passers-by and other people with dogs if they had ever seen him before. The reply was no.

We left the park and guess who followed. I stopped in the police station down the block from my house but they said they would only take him to the pound. That was not an alternative for me. We came out of the police station and abruptly the dog bolted ahead, running down the street, turned, and ran up the stairs of my building. My friend and I looked at each other. When we reached the building I opened the door and he proceeded to run down the stairs to my apartment, as though he'd lived there all his life. What was I going to do with a dog who invited himself in? The dog and I fell asleep together.

Samantha and I finally met. The lecture and music all went well. I told her I needed to talk to her about my new roommate. We would set up a session to talk to "Max." Samantha explained I didn't have to call the new dog Max, but, if I did, it would begin to trigger his memory from our last time together. Remember my dog had died three years earlier and this dog was about one-and-a-half to two years old.

To find out where he had been that year-and-a-half to two years, Samantha had to communicate with him. He mentally "showed pictures" to Samantha, indicating he had been with a family and his job was to protect and keep people away from the little girl. I gather he did such a good job that they got rid of him, but he still loves kids. He then showed pictures of a man, one who must have kicked the shit out of him because trusting men has not been easy for him. Samantha had to piece all this together but this was his history. He also kept saying he knew I lived near the park; he tracked me down there. I accepted what was said, and he stayed. He's been with me for eight years.

Is There a Time Limit on When We Can or Can't Contact a Dead Person?

Eleanor, the mother of Jennifer, the girl who committed suicide, was also concerned that because of the suicide, Jennifer's life would somehow be "off-limits" for contact. Not a problem. She also thought there might be a time limit on when Jennifer could or couldn't be contacted. Jennifer made the answer very clear and had some backup. After Jennifer had made herself known at the beginning, of the session, her maternal grandmother abruptly stepped in to announce she had helped bring Jennifer over, meaning she had been there during Jennifer's transition. This was Eleanor's mother who had died 30 years ago, when Eleanor was very young. Jennifer, on the other hand, had only been in the *spirit world* for two years. There was no difference in clarity of contact. The wires were still fresh!

The amount of time someone has been in the *spirit world* does not have any effect on making contact; a number of DPs have said this. Other factors have a much more definite impact on contact or communication. There are two more common time spans when living folks experience contact with those who have passed over within three days after death and within the first year. Most contact during both the short period and the year long time occurs during dreams but sensory contact experiences do happen.

I've been told that it takes three days for complete separation of non-physical bodies (called *subtle bodies)* to the physical. You disconnect from your physical body immediately at death but it takes three days for the subtle body material to detach from the physical realm. During this time it's easier for the DP to emulate the physical body using the *etheric double*. The *etheric double* is the subtle body that duplicates the physical body. In appearance, it's a violet-gray substance connecting the body with the soul. It detaches from the physical body at the time of death but it retains the physical characteristics for approximately three days. It's during these three days the living sense—via sight, smell, or experiencing other phenomena—those who have just passed over.

I have been assured by the DPs that they have the ability to show up regardless of whether they have been members of the Society for six days, a few hours, or 40 years in our time frame. It is also often true that the longer souls remain in the *spirit world*, the less they are felt by the living. This is not an indication that their ability to make contact is waning or that they don't love you, it simply means they need to move on to other things in their present state, as must the living.

What Happens If My Relatives Reincarnate Before I Join Them in the Spirit World?

There must be a few folks who believe somewhat in reincarnation because this is one of the most commonly asked questions. If they didn't believe, at least a little, why would they care? People seem nervous that when they get over "there," their DPs will be back "here."

There are no set rules as to when, where, or how we reincarnate, for it is strictly an individual process. The *general* rule for coming back is once every five generations. That's a long time between lives. It's more important to know that if we need to have the presence of loved ones when we pass over, they will be there waiting to bring us over.

Don't be concerned how they'll find you. They will. In the same way that they know when someone is going to come for a séance and they want to be there to make themselves known, they are aware and will be there when you pass over.

Will I Know Them and Be Able to Recognize Them When I Die?

Yes and, as just stated, it's more than likely they will be there helping to bring you over to the other side of life. They will appear to you the way you knew them prior to physical death. They will, however, look "all well again" if they died worn out by illness or hurt by physical trauma. Also, as I said, young children grow up on the other side, but you will still recognize them.

Can You Tell If Someone Is Going to Die?

My responsibility is to receive the information as clearly as I can and then relay that information to the client as conscientiously as possible. I do not believe that a medium has the right to tell a client that someone close to them is going to die. There are those in my profession who give out this information; I think they are wrong.

There are many ways a DP will tell me that someone is sick or possibly going to make the transition. I will then suggest to the client that it may be important to plan a visit home or make sure they are complete in their relationship with this person. The information is important but so is how it's conveyed.

Do We Have Foreknowledge of Our Death?

This comes up all the time in my sessions. The soul knows when it is time to return home. It is not always clear to what we call our conscious mind but, because the soul knows, things will be said and done that are out of the ordinary by those getting ready for transition. When the living think back later about different things that were said or done, they can identify what were, at the time, clues.

The rule of thumb is that children and the elderly recognize it sooner, seem to get better physically and go into remission a few days before. A peaceful coma—by that I mean no nervous movements or apparent agitation—is another sign. Since the soul knows it's going to pass over to the other side, one way of preparing for this is for the person to go into a coma-like state or progress to a peaceful coma right before the transition. Again, this is not to imply everyone who goes into a coma will pass over. Obviously, they don't. The DPs have told me, though, that part of the reason they did go into a coma was to help prepare the loved ones to be left behind for the transition.

Rhonda had been a client of mine for several years. She was a deeply spiritual person who had taught yoga and meditation for years to adults and children. Rhonda was a single mom and was very close to her only child, Brad. In her words, they shared everything.

Brad and his high school classmates had been planning for a year to go to Russia. He had been very excited, learning everything he could about the culture and history.

Rhonda remembers talking about death the week before Brad left for Russia. They frequently talked about psychic experiences (Brad had had an NDE when he was seven years old) and the week before his leaving they also happened to talk about "you don't die." They made a pact that whoever went first, the other one would try and make contact. They had no doubt they would still be connected. True, this isn't your typical family discussion, but at the time Rhonda didn't feel the conversation odd or strange, since they had often talked about the paranormal and spiritual matters.

A spring trip was planned and the class was to stay ten days. The night before leaving Russia, Brad called his mom to tell her how terrific the trip was and how much he was enjoying himself. Rhonda said he sounded great and very excited. That same night, he and a few of his classmates decided to have a going-away celebration. Everyone was drinking Russian vodka. Suddenly, without warning, Brad lapsed into a coma. Everybody sobered up fast, deciding they had better rush him to the hospital.

Brad's friend called Rhonda to tell her what happened. She left immediately that day, the day Brad would have returned home. She arrived while Brad was still in a coma. He remained in a coma for seven days.

Throughout the week Rhonda had continuous dreams about Brad letting her know he was fine. However, Brad never came to consciousness. He died; the cause of death was poisoning.

Is the Time of Death Determined by God or Something Greater?

A part of this question has been answered by other DPs who have passed over from suicide. Yes, there is "an allotted time."

They have also stressed that suicide is not the only manner in which we can go before our time. Overindulgence, misuse of drugs, alcohol, or food, may affect our physical bodies to the point that they no longer can endure the abuse. This is a suicide of another sense and can also result in our transition before the allowed time.

The basic answer is that it is determined by God and your own soul when it is your time to pass over. God, however, has also given us the free will to decide what roads to take and how to live our lives. Anyone who makes choices that alter or change his or her soul's course may join the *spirit world* "before his or her time." However, most of the DPs have informed me that they died in the way and at the time that had been predetermined. Many have also just known it was their time.

Does this sampling—the group of DPs who have come through me—accurately represent the greater whole? It appears to be so, but I honestly don't know. This is a tough field for statistical analysis.

Who Writes the Script?

We do pick how we enter the Earth plane, even choosing our parents. Add to the equation the fact that we are also given free will by God.

This is exactly why there are no set rules and the script remains a work-in-progress. Anyone path is strictly individual. Thank God and the rest of the upstairs unit that we are given all the help along the way we need or will accept. Help that is not interference, rather, help that is guidance.

You, God, and the helpers that work with God, the upstairs team, helped make the decision of your soul's journey. You can think of it in the same way you give lessons or responsibilities to your children. You wouldn't give a two- or three-year-old the same responsibilities and lessons you would give a twelve-year-old. In much the same way decisions are given to the soul when coming onto the Earth plane. There are lessons *here* that cannot be learned anywhere else. Each is given the right vehicles, parents or parent, siblings or no siblings, sex, and cultural and economic foundation in which to learn and grow in the way that is right for that souls journey.

Many people will say that it seems like they are learning the same thing over and over. And they probably are, at least until they get it right.

Is There a Devil?

Most of the DPs have been definite that there was no guy dressed in a red suit with a pitchfork waiting in the wings to greet them. No, there is no devil *per se*. However, there are negative or evil forces lurking in the universe.

Let me further explain. In order to understand where evil lies, we need to go back to the principle of energy. We know energy can't die. If an individual or group of people act consciously to do an evil deed or affect a negative force, the energy involved remains and exists as a negative entity. If an individual soul continues to do evil acts, those acts become part of his or her continuing consciousness until such time as some balance is achieved, or a time when the soul wants to change. It is very possible this could be done over a cycle of lifetimes. The more acts that are done, the stronger the negative/evil force in the world and the stronger its concentration within the originator's consciousness. If the acts are done by a group or mass of people, the force or energy behind it is even greater. So, evil does exist and it is powerful, but only as powerful as the force behind it.

Where does this energy go? We know it cannot die, therefore it exists unto itself. If we consciously choose to tap into that force or energy then we need to accept the results of our actions.

We do not become a goody-two-shoes when we die. Our consciousness, our acts, and our memory of them stays with us. It is not the upstairs unit that influences us to do bad things or draw upon negative energy or forces. It is our free will that does so. We have been given the free will by God, while on the Earth plane, to make choices in our lives. We choose our actions and are equally responsible for them.

Second Chance

And God . . . What About God? If There Is One.

Clients have asked their loved ones, "Is there a God?" and "Are you with God?" The answer to the latter has been yes, but attempts at descriptions by the DPs—have been hard to understand by us on this side.

It's probably safer to refer you to an expert—writer and philosopher William James, as channeled by Jane Roberts who recounted the commentary in *The Afterlife Journal of an American Philosopher: The World View of William James*. As fitting with an analyst and seeker of clear thinking in life, James's words about the afterlife make sense:

> *Nowhere have I encountered the furnishings of a conventional heaven, or glimpsed the face of God. On the other hand, certainly I dwell in a psychological heaven by earth's standards, for everywhere I sense a presence, atmosphere, or atmospheric presence that is well-intentioned, gentle yet powerful, and all-knowing. . . .*
>
> *At risk of understating, this presence seems more like a loving condition that permeates existence* [here] *and from which all existence springs. . . . While I am tempted to say that it moves in waves because of its mobile nature, this is not true. Instead it appears out of itself, at each and every point in the universe. . . . I believe that comprehension of this atmospheric presence is automatically meted out according to the needs and conditions and nature of the perceiver.*

It never ceases to amaze me what happens to people mentally, emotionally, and spiritually when they realize, without a doubt, that they have been contacted by a loved one from the *spirit world*. Only people who possess extremely thick armor have no responses or changed thoughts after a session with their DPs. The experience is intensely emotional and has a profound impact on our fundamental concepts of life, death, and God.

Once we reconnect, once we realize that we did not truly lose anyone, that they may no longer have bodies but can still communicate with us and give us their love, then many things and many connections become possible. Thus begins the opening of the *door* of God. We begin to question and search for so many more answers about our death, mortality, and, yes, even God's plan for us.

Every single person has his or her own relationship and thoughts about God. For some, it's a non-relationship: there is no God. Many people have been taught to believe that God does exist but that this powerful existence concerns only judgment and punishment. That separates us from God. Others are more comfortable with no God, thank you. Still others say, sure God is love, but their version of love is more like a useful friendship.

How we act on these beliefs and how we factor in this new experience of connecting with the DPs is a function of our belief system, upbringing, and culture. It is a very special moment when the presence of God is felt. Some will never feel it or can never admit they have felt it. As humans, many of us need everything to be proven. God doesn't always work that way. But these pages are not the place for abstract debate. What is important is that something happens to almost every person seeking to make contact with a loved one who has passed over and who contacts that loved one through me: they find God, or they feel a sense of something greater affecting their lives in a way never realized before. When we discover that a loved one whom we thought had died, in fact did not die and is in touch with us, the door opens. It may only be a crack but it is open. Those seeking answers will begin to test and want to push the door open even more. For the first time, some may question, "What is God?"

I believe there is a God. I *know* there is a God. But many of the most deeply religious people consider my source of information suspect. So my job is not to convince you, but to share with you the information as received.

No one will ever be able to completely convince you that you don't die, or that you can communicate with loved ones after death. Nor can anyone convince you that there is something greater. You have to come to this by yourself. We were given free will to find our own paths, in the ways harmonious to us. When it happens you'll know it and then no one will be able to convince you otherwise. They may call you nuts but they won't change your mind.

Do The Right Messages Always Get Through?

One of the questions I'm asked most frequently by those who are trying to communicate with a loved one who has passed is whether they can be sure the person they're trying to contact will "come through" for them. Sometimes their concerns are practical in nature: "My little girl was only a year old, she wasn't even talking, how will she be able to communicate with me?" Or, "Great Aunt Tillie only spoke Russian, and you only speak English, so how will you know what she's trying to say?"

In these instances, I can assure the questioners that what they perceive as barriers won't hinder their contact. If a child is too young to speak, there will always be an older family member with him or her to provide validating information so that the parent will be certain to recognize the child. And, for reasons I truly can't explain, when Aunt Tillie needs or wants to communicate through me, she will miraculously become fluent in English.

Aside from these practical assurances, however, I can't ever guarantee who will come through in any given situation. That decision is really up to the DPs themselves. In Shakespeare's *King Henry IV, Part One,* Glendower tells Hotspur, "I can call spirits from the vasty deep." And Hotspur replies, "Why, so can I, or so can any man; but will they come when you do call for them?" For my part, the answer is, *not always.*

It may simply be that a particular DP isn't available for contact at the particular time you want to reach him. You may, for example, want to make contact with your father, but he may, at that moment, be too distant to pick up the information. In such a case, he just wasn't meant to come through at that particular moment. Or, there may be other impediments to the communication.

A person might be harboring negative emotions, such as resentment or jealousy, that would hinder the contact.

Or, one of the dead folk might realize that a particular person is not yet ready to receive his message.

Sometimes a DP knows that his or her loved one is not the best person to receive his message, and he'll pick someone else—someone he knows will be willing to listen—to deliver the message for him. The following letter explains how this sort of thing happened to a client of mine who had been desperately trying to find a way to contact her 17-year-old son, David.

> *Suzane,*
>
> *As often as I've practiced the meditation that you walked us through the day of the intimate workshop, I was never really sure if I was "getting anything." As you so often talk about, I kept negating most of what I think I saw or heard. I had this preconceived notion that when I saw something in my mind's eye it wasn't clear enough, or too clear, so none of it could be real. You took us through the meditation and emphasized that we were not to question what we saw, smelled, or heard. I thought, "Here I go again. I'm going to be the only person in the room to either not get anything or not be able to impart what I think I got." I was also thinking that we were wasting all this time and all I wanted to hear was that David was around. But I went through the meditation. Suddenly, the face of a little boy appeared. I knew he was approximately four years old. I also knew more than I saw that he had brown hair and very blue eyes, and that he wanted me to "Tell Mommy*

I love her." As you instructed us, I wrote all this down. One by one, we each gave the information we had "supposedly" received. There was another woman in the room who said she had a friend who was not present who had lost a son named Kevin. You validated this connection with more information.

A couple of weeks later I was driving home and, as I often do now since the loss of my son, I turned off the radio and just let my mind clear. I was in that state of mind and clearly the name "Katie" and then your name, "Suzane Northrop," came to me. Remembering what you'd said, I just went with it and those two names kept coming to me. I thought, "Hot diggity dog, Suzane's DPs are coming through me. When I get home, I'm going to just leave a message on her answering machine and see if she has a relative named Katie."

When I arrived home, I only had 15 minutes before I had to leave for a meeting at Compassionate Friends, a wonderful support group for people who have lost children. So I put off the phone call until later. At the meeting, there was a young woman I'd never seen before talking about how a friend of hers had gone to a psychic a couple of weeks before and, though she knew nothing about psychics, her friend had relayed to her that someone in the room had said they'd seen a little boy about four years old named Kevin and to "Tell Mommy I love her." The woman said that although she really didn't put much stock in the "psychic stuff," she couldn't help believe that this was her son. Another woman in the room said, "Katie, what's the psychic's name?" Katie replied, "Suzane Northrop."

I just about fell off my chair. I shared with Katie after the meeting that I'd been the one who'd had a connection with her son. She had a button on her blouse with a picture of Kevin on it, and I was stunned by how similar he looked to what I'd seen, especially the "very blue eyes." Katie threw her arms around me and through tears thanked me profusely. I was completely overwhelmed that I'd been able to give her a moment with her son again.

I truly trust now the conversations I have in my head with my son and I seldom question the things I experience during meditation, or that happen daily, as they are significant of my son's continued presence and love in my life.

— Mollie

As Mollie's experience shows, the DPs will go to any lengths to get their message across, but they also understand that a direct line to their loved one may not always be the best way to do that. Sometimes it's actually more effective for them to engage in a kind of "psychic telephone tag." In this case, Kevin not only delivered his message of love through Mollie, whom he knew would convey it to his skeptical mother, but in doing so, he also validated Mollie's own belief that her son, David, had remained a continuing presence in her life.

The Last Question: Why?

We cannot bring our loved ones back but knowing they didn't die can help our healing process and, more important, open a door of unexpected possibilities for communication, learning, and forgiveness.

It is possible that a child could reincarnate, into the same family being born as another child. It has happened, however, I'm told it's the exception. If it does happen, it is the child's choice.

Denial of death is the immediate reaction for many. But the respite it brings is temporary and, false. Grief, honest grief, is necessary. The blessing of my work is that my intercession, and the DPs' intercession, can help with the grieving. Contact with your beloved lost one will not diminish the grief. In fact, the grief should be honored. The blessing lies in the beginning of resolution and healing.

Why did God take my only son, daughter, husband, or wife away? Perhaps it wasn't God's doing at all. Perhaps what God did was to give your son or daughter free will to make choices on his or her own. Maybe it was your son or daughter who decided, long before incarnating as your son or daughter, that this lifetime would be short. The issue is not about constant regret or blame or whose fault it was when someone dies. All of this is simply part of the larger program from which everyone must learn.

Maybe our lives constitute a search for truth that each of us must come to on our own. I am told that the knowledge that we don't die helps our transitions in the afterlife. I can only suppose that such knowledge also gives those of us here on earth the freedom to feel less helpless, to understand that there is a greater picture. I hope so. It's why I do what I do.

Chapter 11

Doing This on Your Own

YOU WANT TO TALK TO THEM, YOU KNOW they can hear you, and you want to tell them how much you miss and love them. Are you capable of contacting them yourself? Yes, if you are also capable of hard work and faith. While I fully appreciate the fact that I've been given the very special gift of a heightened ability to *tune into* the vibrations of those in the world of spirit, I also know that everyone of you also has the capacity to enhance your own abilities to connect with that world. We all have untapped depths of knowledge and ability, but it takes training and trust to implement our own inner spirits. You can take the skills and concepts in this chapter to develop clairaudient and

clairvoyant awareness, to understand how communication
with both the *spirit world* and one's own *higher self* happens,
and to make specific, short term contact with the DPs. For
a medium this is a life study.

For successful results at any level, you will need to be
secure in the knowledge that, beyond a doubt, God or a
Higher Power is guiding and protecting you. You'll also
need a realistic perspective on what can and can't happen.

Before discussing exercises and techniques, I want you
to have a clear outlook on one of the most commonly used
methods of contact: the Ouija board.

The Ouija board in and of itself has no power.
However, in using it you give clear access to any discarnate
person who wants to come through, into your mind and
thoughts, including unhappy souls from the Astral realm
or ghosts. It's like inviting someone into your home whom
you've never met and who may stay as long as he or she
likes. Not a bright idea.

An example:

> Richie, a student of mine, called while I was work-
> ing on the manuscript for this book. He left at least
> three urgent messages on my answering machine before
> I had a chance to return his call. When I called him, he
> kept apologizing that he "knew better" because he had
> studied with me, but he now needed my advice. I told
> Richie to calm down and tell me what happened.
>
> He and his girlfriend had started to play with the
> Ouija board a few weeks ago. I asked him, how had he
> gone about it and what did he say? Unfortunately, what
> he had asked was, "Is there anybody who wants to
> come through?" Four spirits showed up immediately.

He was able to talk to them about going into the light and their presence faded. He was ecstatic! He'd learned how to help mixed-up spirits in my classes and now he felt like a savior. Richie was hooked. He then invited a few friends over to show off a little. The board moved like crazy, with several spirits coming through. One was a young man who had died in 1961, at the age of 24, from an accident. He said he had been "lost" for 30 years. None of the spirits, including this young man, had ever seen the light. From the way Richie described this to me I have to assume they were still "in between," probably in Level Two. Richie said that they were all aware of God or a God consciousness but didn't know how to get there or find their way.

Suddenly during this session his maternal grandmother showed up. She had died twelve years ago, and Richie adored her. Richie asked her if she could help the other souls go into the light. It worked. However, something else happened. When the other lost souls came through, one more followed. He described himself, gave his name, when he died, and where he lived while on Earth, and how long he had been where he was. He also made it very clear he was not one of the good guys.

When Richie asked the spirit where he was, he spelled out "H-E-L-L" on the Ouija board. This spirit wouldn't leave. He enjoyed the power he was getting from Richie and having over Richie. Richie's behavior was becoming erratic, angry, even violent. This was not like him and his mother and girlfriend were becoming afraid of what might happen.

Richie called in a panic not knowing how to get rid of the spirit. I told him quite frankly that it wouldn't be easy since he had allowed and encouraged him in. I explained that because of Richie's religious background, the entity knew quite well his fear of Hell. It is not for me to say whether a Hell of any particular format does or does not exist, but negative energy certainly does. I told Richie that the entity would use any means possible to prey on his fears. After all, this was a battle about power and control. The entity knew very well where Richie's weak points were.

Malevolent energy of this level is like a leech. It feeds on the fears of people. The painful part was that Richie let him in. First, by using the Ouija board and then because he said, "Does anyone want to come through?" Both very bad mistakes.

I told Richie that I don't do exorcism or get rid of the bad spirits, but I could make a few suggestions. Since his grandmother had helped the other lost souls go into the light, why not enlist her help to rid him of this negative spirit?

I also suggested that he do the following, to work on the surrounding energy.

Pray, pray, pray. Asking God to change the energy and light to protect him and his home. The darkness must be replaced by "the light." He needed to turn the energy around from fear to faith. This essentially dissipates the negative power.

Keep lighting white candles. This would reinforce the God energy and allow him to focus on prayer and meditating.

Smudging. The burning of herbs is common among Native Americans. The purpose is to cleanse the energy.

I told him not to expect overnight results but to be patient and focus only on God and the light. And do not use that board again! Richie had removed his God-given gift of protection.

God has granted you natural protection by allowing only those you permit to contact you, through your thoughts or mind. I believe that this is one reason that contact for most people is so difficult, that this is God's way of protecting you from any contact outside of the light or contacts attempted without permission. What seems an obstruction is in fact a protection. This is not a game!

Expectations

One of the most common illusions about how the dead folks communicate is that they just show up, "materialize," hover a bit, and have a chat with you. This has happened, but is the least likely manifestation. The DPs are aware this type of appearance might terrify as well as impress the living. I'm told it's also the most difficult method for them. Their primary desire is simply to let you know that they are fine, not dead, and that they will be with you when it's your time. They don't usually need to do or say more, although you may want more.

In a séance, a medium will be the relay point through which the DPs will send messages to you. However, "Tell him yourself; he'll hear you" is a fact. Your loved one is able to hear you. You can do some of this on your own but you'll need to remember that communication with a person in spirit is different in method and components. Audio signals, guided images—not long conversations, most often not even full sentences. Therefore, in order for satisfactory communication to happen you will need to work on developing some very different skills. The following exercise is your beginning point. Some advice: the Step Three preparation may not be easy for you, so practice this ahead of time. Don't worry about the dead folks, they are ready, willing, and very able to communicate. It's up to you to get the rust out of your fine tuner.

Solo Contact: Your Basic Exercise

STEP ONE

Set up an *appointment* with the dead folks. Yes, however odd it sounds, do it—set up an appointment. You may request a certain DP by name (although others you love or who love you may show up anyway). Be specific in setting a time, day, week, and hour. It should be a time when you're not likely to be disturbed or feeling anxious about doing other things. Make a commitment to them and to yourself that you have dedicated this time and place for communication to happen. And you'll have to commit to doing this for a period of at least seven weeks, so don't start when you know you'll be on a business trip or at your cousin's wedding at this time week after next.

The choice of time is up to you, but some time frames have proven to be more naturally conducive: when there is no interference or activity and very early in the morning, if you are a morning person, or at 9 P.M., 11 P.M., or midnight if you are a night person.

When you have decided on a time, you will need to repeat it once or twice, either out loud or silently, "Tuesday at nine o'clock for the next seven weeks I'll be open to receiving communication from . . ."

Step Two

Find yourself a favorite chair and place and assign this as the place you'll be at the time given for the next seven weeks. Committing yourself to the specific place as well as time reinforces your state of receptivity. Remember you have made a promise: You have sent out thought waves to the DPs that for the next seven times in a row, at a certain time, you will be in a receptive state of mind.

Step Three

Mental preparation. This takes place on the set day, anywhere from five to 15 minutes before the appointment. It's not necessary to wear any special clothes, burn incense, or even burn candles unless any of this gives you a sense of peace and helps center you.

Centering and a calm state of mind will be important. You shouldn't be either full from a meal or hungry, nor should you be distracted by what is going on around you. This time is for you. Several minutes before your appointed time, take the phone off the hook, go to your chosen place and either send anyone else around to another part of the house, or have them go somewhere else. Animals, though, usually are not a problem; they will always want to be in the room with you during this state of peaceful relaxation. They are attracted to this state of calm energy and will not disturb you.

Even if alone and determined to be relaxed, you may find this process difficult. Being quiet and listening with your inner ear is hard to sustain. Random thoughts will keep reoccurring and interfering. Acknowledge them, let them go, and return to the focus of being quiet and waiting. This state of relaxation is essential in recognizing and listening to God and your higher self. It's also good for you. Once this becomes easier for you, there are several changes you can expect.

You may need to experiment with various relaxation or meditation techniques to find out what works best for you. Some people want or need music; others find repetitive reciting of a prayer or words effective. Please, read the section on "going inside" later in this chapter and then practice this process as much as you can before the appointment.

Once relaxed, with the phone off the hook, in your favorite chair, wearing your most secure, comfortable clothes, you are ready.

STEP FOUR

Visualization and prayer. Picture yourself surrounded in white light. It doesn't matter how you get the light around you-draw it, feel it, use an image of the moonlight, whatever works. Repeat quietly to yourself, "Only with God's grace and allowance, those loved ones may come through." At this point you "seal" the light and the permission with a prayer. I use the Lord's Prayer or the Twenty-third Psalm. If you prefer to keep God out of this, request permission of *Spirit* or the *Universal Consciousness* that what will happen will be for the highest good, and then invoke whatever words bring you peace of mind.

Feeling the white light surrounding you, feeling yourself safe and protected, begin deep diaphragmatic breathing. Feel/see/imagine yourself surrounded by light, gently and quietly lifting, as if you were in a balloon or spacious elevator. As you feel yourself lifting, consciously leave behind the day's worries and doubts. Affirm that God has made this moment special for you and the one whom you wish to contact. Know that you are opening the door for communication with those loved ones in the *spirit world*.

Feel yourself gently being lifted higher and higher, moving toward a door above. The door opens. See yourself step out, then walking through the door. Before you is a golden field of flowers, tall grass surrounded by trees, sunlight filtering through. Feel that you are warm, protected, and loved.

Looking across the field, you notice a bench. Be aware of what the bench looks like and concentrate on who is sitting there, waiting. Visualize walking toward the bench. Who is there? Your mother, father, sister, son or daughter—someone is waiting to be near you. Allow your emotions to flow. What are you feeling? You may see the person clearly at once or you may not. Sit down on the bench. Do you feel the presence of someone nearby? Do you feel the love that is touching you?

If you do not sense or see the person, do not become worried. You know somehow they are near. You hear a word with your inner ear. It may only be one word. You may not know what it means, but that doesn't matter for you will remain quietly confident that later it will have meaning.

If you can see the other person, sit together and look into each other's eyes. If you hear a familiar voice, say nothing, listen. If you feel an embrace, a quick touch, be still. Know that this moment will stay imprinted in your mind. It is a time given to you both to share and to heal. And know that as the time draws near to leave, you can come to this place again, it will be there when you need it.

After what may seem like a short or long while, you become aware that it will be time to return to your balloon or elevator. For a last moment, feel, see, or sense the presence of your loved one. Within your thoughts, tell yourself and them that it is time to say good-bye and for you to begin the return to outer consciousness. You stand up, sensing that the other person is no longer with you.

Gently and quietly concentrate on the feeling of fulfillment. Once again see yourself walk leisurely back through the field, knowing in your heart that this is your place, your place to return, anytime you want to talk or just feel the presence of your loved one.

You step once again into your *place of light*. It sways but supports you securely. Gently it comes back down. The white light begins to fade but some stays, wrapped securely around you. You see yourself stepping out of the balloon. When the moment is right you'll see and feel yourself coming back into normal consciousness. You will feel relaxed, even if you are not sure of exactly what happened or if you made contact. You will be conscious of feeling love in a way you have never felt before. Stay with that sensation of love for a moment.

STEP FIVE

Pick up your pen and write down all that was said and felt. It doesn't matter how little or how much happened.

This is not about quantity of information but about empowering your relationship.

Don't despair if you think nothing happened. Analyze what didn't happen: No contact? You saw or felt no one? You have six more weeks to venture. No white light? Practice the imagery a few times to get used to it. No relaxation? Practice the deep breathing and focused quiet. No time? Make the time. You missed an appointment? The dead folks will wait. They love you.

AFTERWARD

Don't be surprised, if on the next day or within a few days after your initial endeavor, your inner ear "hears" thoughts suddenly containing a message from the DPs. This often happens when least expected. If it occurs too quickly or you're not sure what that odd sensation or thought was, let it go. It will come back more clearly next time.

Communication can be done both with and without doing this first exercise. The exercise is simply a way to help you make your solo contact. If we give up trying to make this contact, or are afraid of it, we run the risk of closing a vital passageway to God and the route to those who have passed over. My hope is that you'll discover that the DPs, the speakers in spirit, communicate with you in a multitude of ways that most of us aren't ever aware of.

But suppose you feel blocked and the only communication going on is frustration with yourself. If this exercise doesn't work for you, even when repeated, let's examine the possibilities:

CONFLICTS: INNER AND OUTER

Issues, fears, or religious beliefs may slow your progress. Strongly felt emotions, too, can cloud the connection. For some, trying to make contact with loved ones "over there" will be the most difficult process they've ever attempted. For others, it will feel like going home, a feeling they've known their whole life but were not able to share or describe in words.

To whom do you tell? Maybe no one. I believe, and have learned somewhat painfully, that you cannot share the wishes of your heart or the goals of your mind with everybody. Even those closest to you may feel threatened and amused or simply unable to accept any of this. Some truly mean well; for others, what you are doing comes too close to their own fear of death. They say to you, "You are only doing this because you can't accept the death of so and so, and you want to believe they didn't die." This is a very private and personal matter, just as is our relationship to God, something else that often cannot be shared. If you find supportive listeners, hooray for you! Because it's also true that many people who are trying this, or have gone to séances, are stunned at how receptive family and friends can be. Test the water on this before jumping in.

If you do not believe in God, or a *Higher Power*, it may add another level of difficulty. It's very important that you feel protected, guided, and secure that only with God's permission and guidance is any of this possible. Feeling that love and protection will reinforce your trust to open the door to communication.

The act of opening that door creates another layer of problems. Do you believe you have the right to open that door and communicate? Yes, you do. That communication benefits not only you but those who have passed over. There is no evil element inherent in this.

You may also have to accept that contact may happen only once or twice, just enough that the DPs are able to let you know that they are fine until you see them again in the next life. That may be all they need, but this is upsetting for most of the living to accept. Once the door is open, and we know we have been given a message or felt the presence of a loved one, we always want more. However, this may not be possible. We may have to let go and let them move on in their world as we must in ours.

This can be disquieting for those who have waited a long time to make a connection. When that connection is made, if they then have to accept that it may not happen again, most do not understand. Why must the contact be cut off?

I don't know why. The answer lies somewhere between God's compassion and the path chosen for both you and your loved ones. If it's necessary for your growth and theirs that contact stop, then it will stop.

I tell you these things not to disillusion or disappoint you, but to let you know what to expect. A happier extreme is also possible: Once communication is begun, the dead folks may keep showing up in spirit for birthdays, holidays, and weddings. And births, dead folks are big on births!

THE NATURE OF THIS KIND OF COMMUNICATION

Here is the scenario: the brain acts like a miniature radio tuning into different frequencies and vibrations. Essentially, we want to tune into the frequencies where the dead folks are. You and the DPs are in or on different vibrations or frequencies. You must raise your level of pitch or frequency and they must lower theirs in order for communication, to take place. You will hear the message and information through your own mind. It will be their presence or words that are felt but your mind is the receiver. What your frequency can sustain is what will come through. Only those asked for, and in a manner you are capable of handling, may be allowed to come through.

These odd-frequency messages come into the brain quickly, making it difficult to hold on to your first impressions of the feelings or the words received. Everyone has had the experience of walking, cleaning, or performing routine activities and at the same time daydreaming when something or someone flashes into your thoughts. As quickly as it comes, if you are not aware, the image or sensation may slip away. It is in this state of mind where inspirations, ideas, *and* contact with the *spirit world* take place.

What happens for most people is that at the moment they know that they've had communication, the right brain gets pushed aside by the left brain, which comes rushing in to discredit that any message was received or that anything at all happened except that we were behaving foolishly. End result: logic says nothing happened, I made it up.

You must keep reminding yourself that conversation

with dead folks is a non-linear, non-active, primarily non-verbal receptive process. It involves your right brain or intuitive side. For success, you have to get your left brain out of the way. Can you send it away, like getting rid of the kids? Yes, the relaxation technique will help with that.

ONE MORE REASON

There is a final reason why perhaps nothing happens for you during your attempt at communication or in dreams. At that particular time, the communication is just not meant to be. Not forever, but not for now. If that is the case, it is in the hands of God. That's a sad truth we may not want to hear, but, usually, it is the exception; most of us, almost always, will make some form of contact.

Awareness Enhancement

Be patient with yourself. This may be very new for you and many disturbing emotions, resistance, and conflicts may come up. Be honest with yourself. Deal with your fears and beliefs. You don't have to solve them, just acknowledge that you have them. Remember, challenging fears or beliefs is healthy; constantly analyzing and rationalizing them is not.

Give yourself a chance and maybe lighten the atmosphere a little by trying other techniques that may make the going easier for you. Some are fun, some very serious; what is important is what works best for you.

GOING INSIDE

You can communicate with the *spirit world* without knowing or caring about whatever your "higher self" is. But that would mean missing a great opportunity: to discover your higher/better/inner and more interesting self. Besides, in making contact with the *spirit world*, you will be using your higher self anyway. It's the part of us that links us with the God consciousness. The time-honored way to obtain this knowledge of ourselves has been through consciously directed "inner work," such as praying or meditating. The techniques may be focused or may let the mind drift; the goal is the same.

Some consider prayer the Western approach and meditation the Eastern approach. But don't get lost in a bog of spiritual technocracy. What is necessary for prayer and meditation to work is that each individual makes a commitment of discipline and follows through with the teachings that are most comfortable. You should also know that you need not adhere to any dogma, doctrine, or philosophy.

There are many ways to God. Your first attempts at prayer, or trying it again after years away from it, may feel awkward, even slightly ridiculous (*"I wonder whom I think I'm talking to . . . Is anybody there? Does anybody care?"*). Meditation seems even weirder to a lot of people.

Prayer usually has a variety of goals. One is to check in with God. Other goals are to ask, to plead, to thank, to honor. If your goal for prayer now is to begin the communication with consciousness, prayer will naturally lead into a meditation process.

There is no right or wrong way to meditate. If my students were forced to get into this particular position or use that particular mantra, they would probably never be able to meditate. Zen Buddhists (a school of Buddhism) chant the word *Om*, which fires up their spiritual centers. Non-Buddhists may chant a word or phrase because it helps them concentrate. Music helps some people and others need silence. What is imperative is consistent, daily discipline to still the mind. Most of us are creatures of habit; therefore, this must be part of our daily lives, like bathing or brushing our teeth.

Create a space within yourself where you can go. Create an area of peaceful space around you. Begin with five to ten minutes. Later, a longer amount of time will be more desirable. If sitting still seems almost impossible, relax, you'll get there. A lot of this book is about what isn't impossible.

Once we have begun the meditative process we will be automatically "tuning up" or activating spiritual/psychic centers. The spiritual/psychic centers I'm referring to are called *chakras*. In Sanskrit the word means wheels. When we meditate or pray we are activating spiritual energy. This energy travels the route of the chakras and from the base of our spine up through to the base of the brain where all paranormal/psychic activity occurs. This is the reason for activating this energy. Getting it moving will activate the centers responsible for more in-depth psychic awareness.

There are actually 21 minor points and 49 subsidiary points having to do with energy located throughout the body. If you have ever seen a chart of the body in an office of a chiropractor, physician, or therapist who does acupuncture or acupressure, you will see these points indicated in red throughout the muscular-skeletal body structure. The chakras are the seven main points connected to opening up clairaudient and clairvoyant awareness. I want to make a note here: in reciting the Lord's Prayer during and before meditation or prayer you are directly activating the seven spiritual centers, the chakras, or seals. There is a considerable body of lore on the seals (and veils) from the Book of Revelations.

Beginning meditation often brings up particular fears. A common one is anxiety or loss of control. Another is *I'm afraid that a bad spirit will possess or take me over.* I would rather you not attempt meditation or any of the psychic techniques, although they are simple and quite harmless, than attempt something that might amplify your fears even more. I believe there are techniques everyone can do on their own to open up the door to their higher selves. You'll find the one that is right for you.

PSYCHOMETRY

Psychometry is the art of receiving impressions or vibrations by holding on to an object. We do this all the time and are unaware of it. Every time we pick up something that belongs to someone else, we are not just picking up the object but the vibrations of the person or persons to whom it is connected.

Now that may not mean anything to you at first, but think of it this way: let's suppose you buy or are given a piece of jewelry that belongs to someone else—an antique. You begin wearing the jewelry and for no reason start feeling depressed or anxious. More than likely you are not going to attribute these feelings to the new ring or earrings, but still, for no apparent reason, you are having uncomfortable feelings. You don't understand because everything is going all right for you in your life. You happen to take the jewelry off and the feeling goes away. By now you still may not make the connection to the jewelry unless you happen to link these feelings to the times when you wear the jewelry.

Everything has a vibration or life, even rocks. It may not be bad, just bad for you. There probably is nothing wrong with the jewelry itself, but whomever it belonged to was either unhappy or has/had an energy pattern radically different from yours.

This often happens in my classes when someone is holding a piece of jewelry belonging to someone else. For instance, one student picks up an object, a ring that belongs to another student. The owner of the ring is very reserved, private, perhaps secretive. The student holding the ring is open and carefree. These are extreme personalities, and, because of this, the more easy-going person holding the ring might interpret the feeling from the object as cold, insensitive, and aloof. The owner may not be cold at all, but that may be the overreaction of the ring holder.

Someone who is exceptionally calm, holding a ring belonging to someone who is high-strung, could interpret the emotion of the ring owner as very nervous or agitated about something, when, in fact, it's just their high-wired personality. When you are "in" another person's vibration or energy and it is contrary to or different from yours, you may easily misinterpret what you are receiving as bad. It's not bad, just different. This is just one of the possible problems in differentiating and clarifying information you are receiving.

What do you do if you have to wear the jewelry? If your fiancé gave it to you and his mother is coming, or your Aunt Maude gave it to you and she's coming? Putting the jewelry in sea salt for a few days (an old tradition for cleansing) should eliminate the problem. If the feeling continues I would not wear the jewelry at all, or only for short periods. So keep the dinners with your fiancé's mother short.

Psychometry in a Group

Choose an object that belongs to someone else in the group or to someone who is known to a person in the group. If the purpose of this exercise is to get information from a DP, the object should have belonged to the DP. Close your eyes, feel the shape, and sense the significance of the object in your hand. Most often the information will mean nothing to you, which is to be expected, since what you are picking up is information "belonging" to someone else. Sometimes you may never be sure. In a group, you can check with the person who owns the object or brought one from his or her DP.

You can't do this in the same way on your own because you won't get the feedback. You may get very strong, intensely emotive sensations but not know the cause. Be careful. Be careful, too, when trying to "read" an object of some other living person. Why? Well, the worst-case scenario is that he or she might have a disturbed personality.

Basic ethics present another case: when contacting DPs, it is important that only with God's permission is the contact possible. In tuning into a person's vibration you are in the same position; we don't have the right to enter a living person's vibration without his or her permission. In order to have this permission outside of a guided class situation it's best you do this exercise either with a friend, family member or within a group you know.

PICTURE READING

There are a variety of ways this can be done. You can do this exercise by yourself or in a group. Let's focus on the group first.

Within a group, everyone brings a photograph in a sealed envelope. All the envelopes are put into a basket. Each member chooses an envelope brought by someone else. First, hold the envelope in the palm of your hand with eyes closed and feel what information you are receiving, just as with psychometry. Let the thoughts and words flow freely as you express aloud what information you have picked up. Then open the envelope and look at the picture. Again let your feelings flow and try to describe what you feel as you look at the photograph. Ask yourself: how are the feelings different as you look at the photograph from those you felt when your eyes were closed? Was one way to receive the information easier or more difficult than the other? It's sometimes difficult to explain what we are feeling or articulate not-quite-understood differences, but be as clear as possible.

If you are trying to get information on a DP, you should look at a photograph of the person now in spirit. Yes, it does matter if there is more than one person in the photograph because you'll probably pick up feelings for all the people in the photograph. You'll get the sensation of the particular person you are interested in plus sensations from the others as well as the effect of the relationships of those pictured to one other. Try, if you can, to get a photo of one person. If you can't, then just relax, "take in" and express all the data you're getting. It isn't a crisis if you allocate the information to all the wrong persons in the photo. What is important is that the pieces of information that you received are in themselves accurate. You will have to rely on feedback for that. Later on you can fine-tune your gifts. As a medium, I know how hard all the sorting out can be.

There are a number of ways for you to do this exercise on your own. First, go through your own photographs, picking out at least 10 or 15. Put each of the photographs in a separate envelope and then put all the photographs in their envelopes in a basket in front of you. Reach in the basket and pick out an envelope. Hold the envelope in your hand and let your thoughts and feelings go, trusting what you are feeling and the images you are getting. Ask yourself, how many people are in the picture in the envelope? Male or female? Do you get a sense of hot or cold? Do you get a sense of color or seasons, initials, or a framework of time? You may want to write the data down or speak into a tape recorder. Be particular. Give yourself time. After you are satisfied that you have received all the images and information possible for you at this point, you may open the envelope and look at the picture. In looking at it, do you receive any other sensations?

Become quiet and try the exercise once again with another envelope and photo. Two attempts are enough for one session. Afterward, try not to fuss about how much you did or did not receive.

For another variation: You and a friend both put ten to 15 photographs in an envelope and exchange the envelopes. Do this alone or separately. Later, get together and share what each of you picked up from the photographs. You can also do this same type of exercise without photographs. Using color symbols, numbers, stars, crescent moons, or geometric shapes drawn on cards may be easier.

TELEPATHY

Many people have telepathic experiences. You will be thinking of someone perhaps for no particular reason and then, suddenly, the phone rings and it's that person, or you will be thinking of someone and receive a letter from them soon after. People who are extremely close *to* one another tend *to* have telepathic communication all the time. Telepathic exercises often are the most difficult for people *to* do, but, if nothing else, they can be fun at a party.

Set up the group in couples, one person to be called the *Sender,* the other the *Receiver.* The Sender's responsibility is to mentally visualize and concentrate on thinking about the image they are sending. The Receiver then writes down what impressions he or she is picking up. If you are doing this as a game, you can have fun sending all kinds of things but common images *to* use are numbers from one through ten, colors, types of furniture, animals, names of famous people, historical events, and signs of the zodiac.

Then reverse the roles. The Sender becomes the Receiver and vice versa. Whoever is leading the group determines which person in each couple seemed *to* be the better Sender or Receiver. This is done by calculating who scored the most right impressions in receiving or sending.

Next, the better Senders go somewhere private and decide what as a group they want *to* send. The Senders return to the room. Each team sits opposite each other. The Senders collectively focus on the image they are sending. The Receivers then write down the impressions they are mentally getting from the Senders. I think you'll find yourselves happily surprised at how many correct images are transmitted. Either way, it's great fun and one of the few psychic techniques I'd ever recommend as a game. You'll like the next one, too.

SENSORY TELEPATHY

Divide the group into two sections. One part of the group sits behind the other so that those sending are not seen by the Receivers. Each Sender is working with a single Receiver, who sits behind the sender.

The focus will be on the senses involving smell, taste, and touch. Each particular Sender within the group of Senders individually places something with a strong smell under his or her nose while the Receiver tries to telepathically smell what the Sender is sending. Many odors are easily picked up so the taste or touch exercise might be more of a test. The Senders put the taste objects in their mouths: honey, cinnamon, Tabasco sauce, or anything with a strong taste. For touch, work with shapes (dull, sharp, or round, such as utensils or sponges) or temperature.

The fun aspect of all these techniques doesn't negate the fact that they are powerful, positive tools to help you enhance your sensitivity. Be patient, especially with telepathy, which is probably the most difficult to do as a conscious exercise. However, if you are really getting mad at yourself or frustrated, switch to another method. You don't have to do everything. This final exercise may be the most beneficial.

PRAYER CIRCLES

Yes, prayer-again. Prayer is always something you can do by yourself. However, there is power in numbers. Prayer with visualization will help you focus on sending protection to those you love, whether DPs or living.

I've always ended my classes and workshops with a prayer that is shared together. It's really quite simple, just as prayer should be. We gather in a circle holding hands. Each person then verbally releases into the circle a name or circumstance to which they want to give energy and healing. The words are then repeated by the group: *peace on earth, light,* and *love* to family members, friends, and animals.

One evening during a prayer circle, a student of mine, Ellen, asked that her mother be given healing and love. She told us her mother would be having heart bypass surgery the next morning, but she didn't tell us that she and her mother had had their share of problems. Two weeks later, Ellen came to class overjoyed.

A few days after the operation her mother had a dream. In the dream she saw Ellen praying for her to be well again. She confronted Ellen, was this true? Ellen replied, yes, very reluctantly. "Oh mom, I put your name in the prayer circle at the end of class and asked that you be well and everything go okay." This was awkward for Ellen to admit because she was sure her mother would ridicule her.

Her mother responded, "Ellen, I saw you so clearly in the dream sending me love to get well. It made me feel miserable. I've missed you. Can we stay over?"

LISTEN OUTWARDLY, LISTEN INWARDLY

Have you noticed that all these techniques are simple? That they ask you to have both a sense of humor and a willingness to open the doors that lead to your carefully protected inner self, those closed doors that have been keeping out the drafts of other people's emotions? Listen to what you've not had time to hear before. Listen outwardly, listen inwardly. You'll gain as a person, you'll gain as a spouse or true friend, you'll gain as a receiver of the DPs' love.

As you increase your ability to do these exercises, you'll increase your faith in yourself, in what you are capable of being, and in what communication is capable of being. And that's what the DPs are waiting for, for you to astonish yourself and say, "Hey, I can do this! It works! Maybe I can do more?"

No one can give you faith. If you lack it, a large chunk of life will be more difficult. Certainly, contact with the DPs will be more difficult. I'm pretty sure we all have some faith, lying around inside ourselves, unappreciated. With rare exception, it is our fears-actually, an accumulation of years of fears-that get in the way of our faith.

Remember the old story: Fear knocked on the door, Faith opened it and there was no one there. Write your own story. Don't be afraid to open this new door. Someone is already there waiting for you.

ONCE YOU'VE BEEN SUCCESSFUL IN CONNECTING WITH THE DPS, either on your own or with the help of a medium, you'll certainly be wanting the messages to continue, and you'll probably assume that if your loved one "came through" for you once, he or she will undoubtedly do so again. And it's certainly possible that this will happen. You may sense a presence particularly on special occasions, such as holidays, birthdays, and anniversaries. But it's also possible that after one or two contacts, your DP won't be there for you again.

I don't know exactly why this happens, but I do know that it happens for a reason. Perhaps your loved one just needed to assure you that he loved you and was still a presence in your life, and having delivered this message, there was no more for him to say. Or perhaps he or she needed to move on with his own soul's growth and evolution, just as you now need to let go and move on with your own. Remember that before you began these contacts, you gave yourself over to the *Higher Power* and avowed that you were acting for the highest good. It's simply not up to you to decide when that good has been accomplished.

Chapter 12

Dreams and Prayers

"MY MOTHER/FATHER/BROTHER CAME TO visit me, it was so real. It's as if they were standing right there. I woke up and knew, without a doubt, that my mother had been with me. This connection was so beautiful and loving I wanted to share it with my sisters/spouse/friend, but when I told them they said, 'No, you just want to believe she was there.'" If you learn nothing else about communication with the DPs, understand two things: 1) a whole lot of people aren't going to believe you made contact, no matter what the format is; 2) not every contact is dramatic.

Most contacts with the DPs happen through *dreams*. This is not to say that every time we dream of someone in the *spirit world* it means they are making contact with us but, if they are, it will happen most frequently and easily through our dreams. Why? Information from the other world comes through our right brain. For this to happen easily, the analytical side needs to abstain for a while. The DPs have to come through in a way in which you can receive them with minimal emotional or intellectual interference and that's easier when we are sleeping.

I feel very strongly about the power of our dreams. Dreams and dream work can greatly help you become more attuned psychically and more sensitive psychologically. With or without the DPs, your dreams give you clues for *you*. The more you use your dreams to work for you, the more they will enhance your ability to understand and deal with life experiences as well as open up doors to the DPs.

How Do We Know It's Real?

The ways we are communicated with and given information in our dreams are as numerous and varied as the dreams themselves. Dreams can be precognitive, symbolic, and quite literal, or all of these. The DPs' messages may as well be quite literal or symbolic.

The type of dream is one clue to its reality as DP contact. For example, people will often dream that those who have passed over are in trouble or mad at them for some reason. These dreams, I've discovered, are most likely expressions of fears or unresolved issues that the living may have regarding the loved one in spirit. You wake up feeling your loved one in spirit is angry at you; the actuality is probably your own deep-seated guilt that you had left things unfinished, words unsaid.

Direct contact is difficult enough to determine; dream symbolism, literally, adds layers of difficulty. If you are searching to find out if your dream is symbolic or contains a DP message, you may appreciate the following technique.

Why Do This Exercise?

All of this is a lot of work. So why are you bothering? I believe this exercise will help clarify whether you are truly being contacted by someone in spirit or whether the dream is delivering a message from your subconscious. On another level, this dream technique is a great tool to help you develop, psychically. In utilizing your dreams to work for you, you will naturally be developing your subconscious mind and begin opening that door to your higher self and the other world.

Going through this exercise will at least "clear the channels," easing many fears or helping you understand some of the unresolved issues you may have. Then maybe the next time you dream about your DPs, they may very well be able to get through to you with greater clarity.

Edgar Cayce, probably the most famous psychic-medium in this century, recounted some 1,700 dreams from people who had specific, validated information from loved ones in the *spirit world*. In his work, as in mine, the most frequent message they wanted the living to understand was that they were at peace, in good health, and the living need not grieve for them any longer. I have developed the dream exercise, but I haven't done any of Cayce's work on serious dream interpretation.

People do keep telling me about their dreams, though. Séance clients have mentioned dreams in the easing-off period of casual conversation after the séance. At a party, when someone finds out I'm a medium, it's almost funny. First they chuckle, then they look uncomfortable, then they confide to me, "I had this absolutely weird dream. You wouldn't believe it." I believe it.

The Dream Exercise

Step One

Quiet yourself, find your center, put aside distraction.

Step Two

Once you become calm, let your thoughts flow freely. Direct them only so far as to "relive" a dream. See yourself going through the dream again, observing and remembering as many details and specific images as possible. Was there a DP present? Did someone in the dream remind you of a DP? If so, keep this in mind, but don't judge or overanalyze. Don't force anything, just go through the dream, letting your thoughts flow. With this relaxed attentiveness, go through to the end of the dream.

Step Three

Go through the dream a second time, but this time experience becoming one of the significant personalities in the dream, as if you were that person. Experience what he or she may be feeling as if the experience was yours. Once you have done this with one person or personality in the dream, then go on to another. It is important to identify each other person and personality as I/me. If the other person is a DP or reminds you of a DP, what you experience by "becoming" the personality may be part of the message.

STEP FOUR

Now, see yourself going through the dream again as yourself, but this time change any detail, sequence or surrounding-anything at all you want to change about the dream. Once you have done this, change the significant personalities in the dream.

As you are making and visualizing the changes, be aware of what emotion or emotions you are going through. Be aware whether the direct changes you are making affect anyone else in the dream. How are they affected? If the dream contains a DP contact, then during the changes, you, as one of the characters in the dream, may get a primary message or experience a great wave of love, a sense of urgency, or a sense of peace—something you weren't expecting. Or you may "see" those same sensations affecting one of the other dream personalities. You will *not* feel guilt or anger directed at you.

Sometimes this process can be emotional but it's always better to experience as much as possible in order to understand all the aspects of the dream personalities, some of which may be reflections of yourself, or reflections of your relationship with the DP.

STEP FIVE

There are two kinds of dreams we are looking at: one dealing with your life issues and the other with DP contact. You need to determine which kind of dream you have had.

For a DP contact there are both subtle intimations and sudden clarities—there are no set rules. There are, however, some markers you may measure against.

If your relationship with a DP has been positive, you will wake up from a contact with the prevalent feeling of warmth and love. If your relationship has been negative, you may wake up in a cold sweat. What happened in the dream may not have been frightening, but the simple dream appearance or some aspect of a dream person that reminds you of the DP may trigger denial, fear, or anger. That may happen even if the DP's message was love.

Negative or positive, you will have felt yourself to be in the presence of the DP. You may not have "seen" them, but one of the personalities or one aspect of a particular personality will be evocative of them. Even if you have not pictured the DP, the experience will be vivid. You may get a message of warning or love. You may simply be told (or experience while "becoming" a personality) that they are fine. You will have to develop your own personal sense of differentiating dreams. Each experience is unique to the individual: some of you will get extremely clear messages, others will have to work to understand less specific meanings.

You can give yourself some help in advance. I suggest to clients and students that before going to sleep, you tell your higher self and the loved one in spirit that you are opening the door for communication to happen. In the end, the big leap of faith may be the determining factor in whether you believe a contact did or did not happen.

If the dream has been symbolic, with messages about your life, this is valuable, too. Review the emotions you connect to the personalities in the dream. Try to determine which personality generates which emotion in you. Is it the entire personality or some particular aspect of the personality? Consider how each of these aspects impacts on you or a life situation that is now affecting you emotionally.

Advisory Dreams

It is amazing how advice we refused to accept from people when they were still alive becomes something we ask for when they pass over. Sometimes the advice from the DPs is highly charged and pertinent, other times it's pretty innocuous. Often we ask for what they cannot give. A workshop student asked about her mother: "Doesn't she know how much I need to hear from her? I need her to tell me what to do!" Well, the DPs can't always do that for you. It is your life and your responsibility to make the choices.

Another client had asked her much-loved brother, now deceased, if he could help her with her job. No, he answered in a dream three days later. "Please don't ask my help in this matter since I can't help you. This is something you have to do on your own." I don't mean to make fun of this, but one of the DPs' messages is: *This is your life, live it.*

Mrs. B had a strong, healthy skeptical side to her but she had had too many psychic experiences after her husband's death to keep the skepticism going. Things started happening in their house: clocks started ticking that had been broken; her wedding band broke, she got it fixed, it broke once more, so she gave it to her daughter and it never broke again. All this activity started to frighten her daughter Beth. Finally, one day Beth yelled out, "Dad I know you want to let us know you're around, but you are frightening me. Would you please stop!" Everything immediately stopped.

Once she started believing in this "stuff," Mrs. B became a little miffed. Her husband came to visit everyone but her. He had visited her sister in a dream, her father in a dream and her son and daughter in their dreams, but not her. In her frustration she said out loud, "I want you to come tonight, give me a sign so I'll know it's you." Presumably, Mr. B got the message because in the middle of the night the entire family was awakened to the sound of shattering glass. Mrs. B's very expensive, very secure chandelier had crashed from the ceiling onto the dining room table. Mrs. B looked at her children, looked toward the ceiling and calmly said to her husband Henry, "That's not exactly what I had in mind!"

Three years went by before she had a dream where he came to her and she wasn't too happy with him then either.

Below is a transcript of her description.

I woke up from the dream very upset. Here I'd been waiting and waiting to hear from him and I expected much more than the message I got! In my dream he was very agitated and insisted that I call an electrician to check out the house. So I did. The electrician began the inspection, he immediately noticed the house had aluminum wiring, standard for houses built during the '60s and '70s but now considered to be dangerous. It meant all the wiring in the house would have to be redone.

This was a tremendous job, people working for days. There are twelve rooms in my house and they had to start at one end, working their way through. The last room to be done was the dining room. As the electrician started removing a screw in a wall plate, a small fire started in the box. He said to me, "I can't believe after living in this house for all these years you suddenly decide to redo your wiring and, while we're here, an electrical fire begins."

"I only did it because my husband insisted," I told him. You can just imagine how this story spread like wildfire amongst all the electricians on Long Island. 'Woman hears message from dead husband that saves house from catching on fire."

Mrs. B, by the way, was one of my all-time favorite clients. Now a member of the DPs, she still remains very dear to me and often stops by to say hello!

※　※　※

Peggy's maternal grandmother came through, insisting there was a problem with Peggy's Aunt Claire. I said, "I feel your grandmother is extremely worried about your aunt. Something has happened and part of the difficulty lies in the relationship between your mother and her sister. Your grandma says they have been like oil and vinegar from day one. I'm certain there is something else she wants you to know about your aunt. She won't leave it alone."

Peggy was a little annoyed. "I'm sorry, I can't help you. I'm just not aware of any problems with my aunt, other than the usual problems with my mother and that's been going on for years."

"Your grandmother insists she's been trying to contact you. Are you aware of this?"

That caught Peggy off guard. She looked a bit shocked, that funny look people get when they think I've read their minds. I don't read minds, I'm not supposed to. I'm only allowed to enter a person's vibration if I have his or her permission.

Peggy finally replied, "Actually, I have been feeling my grandmother's presence exceptionally strong for the last two weeks. I have to admit this was one of the reasons I came to see you. I have also been having vivid dreams about her. I really wasn't sure if there was any connection. I thought maybe she was around because I was going through major changes and transitions in my life."

Her grandmother was in fact not worried about Peggy, her concern was Peggy's aunt and trying to communicate a message. Neither one of us knew what, but Peggy soon found out. Her aunt had suffered a stroke and her mother didn't know about it.

   ✿ ✿ ✿

At a séance in New Jersey, five DPs all seemingly connected to one person came pushing their way through. To make it more difficult, all their names started with the initial D. With the help of Elizabeth (my control) and Patricia, the woman attending the séance to whom the DPs belonged, all the names were unscrambled. They were Patricia's DP siblings: Debbie, Donna, Davey, Dorothy, and, finally, Donald. The Donald and the Donna spirits were the most confusing to receive because they were twins.

Patricia had been the last of seven children and had only one brother who was still living and in Ireland. Her DP siblings had never left Ireland and couldn't quite figure out how Patricia had ended up in the States. Suddenly, two more DPs connected to Patricia came through. One had passed over from a long-term illness connected to the lungs and the other had passed quickly from a heart attack. They were Patricia's parents, Katherine and Patrick.

Patricia's father kept apologizing for an action that appeared to have affected all the siblings after his death. He also seemed proud of something that he had done to resolve the problem. His wife, who up to this time had been silent, berated him, "For four years after you died the entire family was torn apart and in a constant battle due to your stubbornness about your will. You should have never done what you did." Then all the D-names got into the discussion.

I'm told the entire séance group was enthralled, but not until the end of the séance did Patricia reveal the truth of her family's mystery. As I was slowly coming back into consciousness I heard the start of the usual "Was she right about you" questions. Someone who couldn't stand the suspense boldly asked Patricia what was all the fuss about her father's will? Patricia chuckled and explained that her father's will gave exclusive rights to the farm to one brother, Patrick Jr., excluding the rest of her siblings. The will didn't mention her mother, because her father had apparently assumed Patrick Jr. would take care of her. Patricia continued (quotes mine):

"Everyone knew where Dad kept his will, no one ever thought about reading it before his death because we all assumed the farm belonged to the family. Then my father died unexpectedly from a heart attack. The will was read: everything was to go to my brother, Patrick Jr. Patrick, my young, cocky brother, let all of us know it was his farm and he would do with it as he pleased. This did not sit well with my brothers and sisters. For four years my brothers and sisters battled, contesting my father's will.

"Then, four years to the day of my father's death, my sister Dorothy, the first girl born and my father's favorite, had a dream. She woke up, feeling my father's presence in the middle of the night. She waited but nothing happened. When she went back to sleep he came to her again in a dream and told her he had written another will and she would find it hidden in the sole of one of his fishing boots.

"Dorothy woke up, with such a clear and vivid impression of this dream that she couldn't wait to tell my mother. Mother then tried to remember if her husband's boots were still in the shed behind the barn where he kept all his fishing gear. If only the boys hadn't removed them! They rummaged through the shed and found the boots way in the back, right where he kept them, next to his fishing box and pole. They frantically tore the boots apart; there it was, a will dated nine months after the original one, granting the farm to all the family. I guess my father must have felt conflicted enough to change his will."

Everyone in Patricia's family was then happy except Patrick Jr. Everyone at the séance applauded. Patricia's father in spirit was equally happy, although her mother thought that he had, only finally fixed what he had messed up in the first place and she was still telling him so—in spirit!

Precognitive Dreams

Precognitive dreams and precognitive insights are essentially the same. They most often bring contact and insight prior to something happening. The Soul always knows when something is going to happen and will make every effort to give us a message. And the Soul is an ongoing work in progress, so it is continually trying to process what it is experiencing, for its own growth and ours. Contact dreams with loved ones that have *crossed over,* usually come right after or within the first year of that person's passing. There are different levels of the dream state. We can get clarity, understanding and guidance if we learn to pay attention to our dreams.

A time that comes to mind for me is when I had returned one evening from a wake of someone I was connected to by a close friend. On the way home, I started to feel a deep sense of loss that seemed odd. I knew the woman who had died, but there seemed no reason for me to be in this state. What I found myself focusing on was how devastating this woman's husband must be feeling from losing someone he had been with for so many years, and how it would be for him to live without her. (He would prove to be resilient over time, and move through his grief to go on with his life.) Anyway, I came home and remember lying very quietly on the floor. My pet dog, Max, came over to me and I felt the sudden need to pull him close. So, here I am laying on the floor, very emotional, and Max there looking in my eyes as if he knew what I was feeling. Tears came to my eyes.

I want to share with you that I now believe that evening I was having a precognitive insight. Less than a month after that, Max became ill and started to go quickly downhill. He became unable to walk very well and I took him to a vet for examination. It was discovered that he had cancer of the spine. This was April, and, by June 5, Max passed over. I truly feel that in that evening, months earlier, when I lay on the floor of my home grieving and wondering how that husband could go on, Max at my side, had been my soul's way of preparing me.

I want to be clear that this all came in a non-dreaming state. I was clearly awake that evening on the floor with Max. The soul knows what's going on and it will start to prepare us for what we are about to experience in our *human* lives. Sometimes we are aware of the messages and sometimes we are not. I didn't understand this one until after Max had been diagnosed as terminally ill. Because the soul had given me its message that evening, it was imprinted somewhere in my knowing about what was to transpire. Therefore, when I did realize Max was ill and would not live long, I could not go into an *unconscious* denial about it. You see, I couldn't just "blank out" because somewhere inside me, I already knew. When the soul has a message to get across, if you don't get it one way, it will find another. There is a place within each of us that connects to that "higher place." And I believe all of you understand the difference between a *knowing* that has a question mark of doubt and a *knowing* associated with conviction. There is no doubt, no wavering on the later kind of knowing. It's solid.

Donna had a dream about her son, Greg. In the dream her son appeared to her drinking and doing drugs. At the time she found this odd: Greg was very much alive and well, and not doing those things. Or so she thought.

Three days after the dream Greg died from suicide, through an overdose of alcohol and sleeping pills. After his death he came to his best friend in a dream to tell him he was fine and well. Greg also asked his friend to please tell his mother he loved her and was sorry.

❦   ❦   ❦

Another client, a staid businessman named Thomas, sat there dumfounded at a séance as his mother-in-law, who died before his marriage, spoke through me (quotes mine):

> "I want you to know I approved of you for my daughter, and actually her father and a former lover here brought you into her life at a point where it was important for both of you. I want you to know that I did indeed visit her. Remind her I told her about the new baby girl you both just had. The child's beautiful and will for sure give you a run for your money."

Thomas was so excited he almost jumped out of the chair. "My wife got up in the middle of the night to take one of those pregnancy tests when she heard her mother's voice say, 'Go back to sleep. You are pregnant with a little girl.'"

❦   ❦   ❦

Mrs. Ottoviani, the mother of my client Anne, had had a reoccurring dream years before she was married. In the dream she would have three children but one of the children would fall into the water and drown. She married and did in fact have three children. She continued to be very fearful of her children near the water since the dream continues to haunt her. Her son, Anthony, married and immediately his wife became pregnant. She was six months pregnant when Anthony had a fatal accident and drowned. His mother's worst nightmare did indeed come true.

There's more to this story. Mrs. Ottoviani had to be hospitalized from emotional exhaustion. Then, one night, Anthony came to her in a dream and told her, "Mom, even though I'm here it's like I'm still there with you. But you need to stay alive to take care of Dad." This dream visit helped relieve his mother of the stress and pain and she was able to leave the hospital. Her difficulty came back when she mentioned this dream to her priest. No Catholic was allowed to attempt to speak with those who are dead, she was told sternly. A strict Catholic, she took this to heart.

Did her son respect her wishes? I don't know. I only know the DPs won't come without your permission or your desire for contact to happen. The dreams did stop.

Mrs. Ottoviani again went into depression. Her husband threatened to leave her a year after Anthony's death because he couldn't "come home to a morgue" anymore. Anthony then came to his sister Anne in a dream and asked her to let their mother know that he was waiting and would contact her when she overcame her conflict. Anne told her mother and that did it. Her mother decided that even if the Church didn't understand, her son's love was more important. Her visits from him once again increased in her dreams.

During one dream, he told his mother he couldn't stay very long because he had to go help a neighbor, Mrs. Vicci. His mother thought this strange but by now had grown to trust Anthony's visits. The next day Anne came home asking, "Did you know Mrs. Vicci died last night?"

Anthony had been dead 20 years when his father passed away. Anne saw her father in her dreams. In one unusual visit he told her that he *wanted* her to ask for his help because it would help *him* progress in his spiritual growth. When Anne told her mother about the dreams and her father, her mother was hurt. "Why doesn't he come to visit me like Anthony?" "Mom! How would I know?" Anne asked in exasperation. "Probably for the same reason Anthony visits you more than me."

A few months went by and Anne's father came through again in a dream. He told Anne the reason he hadn't come to see her mother was because she hadn't let him go, she was still clutching at his memory. He didn't want to upset her or himself. When she could let him go, he would come to visit her.

This story illustrates two important factors in making contact with our loved ones in the *spirit world*: first, you can't force the contact. It has to happen in its own time. Second, the DPs do not need or want you to let their death take over your life.

What they do need is something so often taken for granted or so often forgotten: *prayers*. Your prayers will surely help.

They Do Need Your Prayers

When you see someone you love crying, especially if you are the reason, you cannot help but feel sad and upset and at fault. That's true for the DPs, too. Your holding on to sorrow or self-reproach will not help them. But your prayers will, for it's your prayers that send them with love on their new journeys.

Dr. Robert Crookall, a British geologist, botanist, and member of the British Society of Psychical Research (BSPR) analyzed numerous communications in his book, *The Supreme Adventure,* and cautioned, "The first wish of the newly dead is to assure the still-embodied family and friends of their [the deceased's] survival and well-being. The second wish usually to entreat the bereaved not to indulge in excessive grief as it may hold back the deceased from progression."

> *You used to sigh, it had an awful effect on me, but I'm getting lighter with you. No sadness. Keep it jolly, or it hurts so horribly.*

— A young DP to his mother

I have always ended my classes with a prayer circle, and it's been shown to me over and over again how powerful our prayers are. When our prayers are offered for someone else-living or dead-we are, with words and thoughts, giving that person or his or her circumstance to God, a *Higher Power.* Words and thoughts are *energy.* The energy inherent in words and thoughts helps bring about the manifestation of our prayers.

A client once asked me, how could she help her son who had been killed during the war. I told her honestly that sending him prayers is the best help a mother could give her son. She replied:

> *It's so funny you should tell me to pray! Right after I had word my son was killed, I sat daily with my rosary beads* [the way she had been taught to pray] *and prayed he was well and in God's hands. Then I had a dream and in the dream my son came to me and said he heard my prayers and thanked me. I've never forgotten that experience. I knew then he was safe and in God's hands. You are the only person I have shared this dream with.*

Mind-body connections have been a focal point of research for over a decade. It's easily understandable that people may get well by praying themselves and knowing that others are praying for them. Research is showing that they may get better even when they are *not aware* that they are being prayed for. Moreover, the person doing the praying needn't be close by. Prayer at a distance, sending prayer energy to someone miles or continents away, will work. Please then believe in the power of prayer over what is conceptually the longest possible distance for us— prayers from this life to the next.

Prayers for the dead are said in every major religion. We are essentially sending them our blessings for going on to a new life in the *spirit world*. Those that have gone over to the other side hear and appreciate your prayers. Don't ever think they don't.

A student once said to me, "I used to pray in church when growing up, but it was just words. I never really understood how important the words were until I spoke them in class with others. We discussed, and felt, the power of the prayers said."

Many think they're above prayer, that it's a crock. Well, they're wrong. "I pray to God, why doesn't He answer?" I assure you, your prayers are answered, maybe not in the way you would wish them to be or you think they should be, but in the way that is probably the best for you and those you have prayed for.

I believe that in order to pray, we probably need to forgive. This is certainly true concerning prayers for our DPs. Prayer is another way of letting go and trusting that even if we don't know why loved ones so dear have gone over into the *spirit world*, it was their time. The more we have difficulty in letting go, the more difficult it is to pray. When a tragedy happens and someone is close to death, if the family members happen to be religious or spiritual, they will pray that God heal the loved one in pain. However, if the loved one dies, those left behind feel betrayed by God, certain that their prayers were not answered.

I've heard so many times from the DPs that if they had lived and stayed on they would have been in a coma or brain dead in useless bodies. They want the living to know their prayers were answered for now the DPs are fully alive in spirit, not burdening the family left behind.

Praying is not about what you want, but what God and the DPs want or feel is best. Send them love and blessings on their new journey; tell them you know they are still with you but that they must go on their path. Acknowledge your deep sorrow and share it with them but without blame or yearning. When a child has to leave home to begin school, it's hard to see that three-year-old leave your side, but it is what the child needs to do. Similarly, your prayers for the DPs give them the added strength to begin to go into the light and toward whatever experiences are next for them.

Death is a transition only and it alone cannot end our love. Our love only ends and closes off when we cannot accept the path now taken by those we deeply love. It is our prayers that truly tell them how deeply we do love them because we are willing to let them go and wish them, "Go with God." They will never truly leave us.

Chapter 13

Getting On with the Rest of Our Lives

As a medium, I live with no exaggeration between two worlds, that of the living and that of the dead; well, at least physically I do. I intercede for the living, who feel death has separated them from their loved ones. The living learn that death has not ended their relationship, that only the physical bond of love has changed. For many, this in itself is deeply painful and they want more contact, more time, more substance. Part of the healing work is to help the bereaved begin to accept both the possibilities and the limitations.

I cannot bring back the physical body to touch or to look at as once before. I can only be the medium, the channel that links and opens the doors for the changed communication to occur.

As my mind and spirit become interwoven with those in the *spirit world*, I feel their love for the living. It is this energy, this force of love that flows through me with each session. It is at these moments that I wish the person sitting across from me could be inside my head to experience the thoughts and feelings that connect me with their loved ones. As the medium, I have to stay once removed and apart from the emotionality. But great surges of emotion, love, and letting go of grief pass through me, between the living and their dearest DPs.

I have bathed in the ceaseless barrage of people's relationships. I "see" such a bigger picture, too-the why's of their lives, their bonds and connections, and the different roads taken. All this continually reinforces for me the imperative that each of us must make it a priority in life to communicate, confront, and understand every level of our relationships. So many people share with me the continual pain of holding on to what was not said to a parent or loved one who died 20 years ago, or even yesterday. I also meet the extreme opposite, people who have harbored feelings of anger and sadness for 20 years because they can't forgive something done or not done, love withheld, or love given to someone else.

The theme of non-forgiveness dominates the next séance.

Four women were welcoming pets and relatives in spirit, but the minute it came to their spouses, the walls went up.

Bernice was the oldest of the group. She had been married to Ben for 30 years and they had three children before he died. She was glad he was dead. He deserved to be dead. Her words were, "Everything he touched turned to crap!" She felt she came from a time and culture where women stuck it out in a marriage no matter what. She stuck it out and was still very angry that she had done so.

She claimed her daughter had had a terrible relationship with the father (I learned separately this was not so). Now she saw all of Ben's shortcomings in her daughter's husband. "Why couldn't she have found someone who wasn't such a loser?" Ben, in spirit, tried to talk to her; she ignored him.

Roz's husband Philip came through asking for her forgiveness, but she was holding on to whatever rage and anger she had toward him. No way was she ever going to forgive him. Philip had been a drinker or, in Roz's words, a drunk. He destroyed everything they had together and had been a rotten husband and father. She'd made sure he hadn't been allowed to see their daughter Sheila. She was glad to say that Sheila still hated her father, and she wouldn't forgive him in spirit either.

Sharon had managed to forgive her husband over the years. Gerald came through in spirit, apologizing to her for the hard times, and regretting he had allowed their daughter Page to put him on a pedestal. Page was angry with her father for dying and was in revolt, Gerald said. She was "acting out" and going with a man her father's age, to make up for the loss of her father. Gerald recognized that Sharon had her hands full. Sharon was thankful that she and Gerald had come to terms before his death, making true forgiveness a possibility. Now if only Page could do the same.

❧ ❧ ❧

Jackie and Lawrence had been living together for five years when he took his own life. He kissed her goodnight, then went into the bedroom and hung himself. Jackie told the séance group that his ex-wife had been making havoc of his life more and more. Jackie and Lawrence had been very much in love, but it wasn't enough in the end. When Lawrence came through in the séance, Jackie told him she realized he just couldn't handle his emotional pain any more, and she did know that his not wanting to be in his body any longer had nothing to do with her.

Two in this group had made peace, two had not. There's very little that I as a medium can do when people consider hatred a comfortable state, except pray that they'll come back for another séance, another contact, and learn something about forgiveness along the way.

Joey's is another story of not being able to let go of hate. Joey attended a séance in New Jersey and, during this séance, his father Alexander showed up. In fact, he came through several times throughout the séance and Joey rudely refused to acknowledge his presence. I probably would never have known the true circumstances if not for his friend Michael, in whose house the séance took place. Michael felt responsible for Joey's recalcitrance during the séance. So, afterward, he took me aside to explain Joey's painful relationship, or lack of relationship, with his father.

Joey's father came through loud and clear during the séance. He identified himself in several ways; his name, when and how he died, the name of Joey's mother, and the name of Joey's son. Joey's wife, also in attendance at the séance, sat there, very upset that Joey wouldn't say anything. She knew Joey's childhood was a sore subject; in fact, she had thought that if his father did come through at the séance it might help Joey confront the struggles with his father. Wrong. Joey refused to acknowledge his father. He wasn't denying the validity of the séance; he did acknowledge his grandparents and relatives on his mother's side who also came through. But he sat, arms folded, denying his father's presence, which made his father try even harder to push his way through. Do you know what it's like to be between a father and son who won't communicate, and, to top it off, one is living and the other one is dead! Alexander only wanted Joey's forgiveness and to tell him that there were things that Joey didn't know and at the time wouldn't have understood. It didn't matter; Joey wanted nothing to do with him.

I remember feeling very exhausted and frustrated. I knew this pattern well; I've seen it so many times. Once again, the dead folks were being the realists and were trying harder than the living to resolve the old pains and obstacles that prevented both sides from healing and moving on. This was one relationship that would have to be worked out in another place and time.

It was late in the evening and the séance was coming to an end. Soon I would have to close the door of communication. It's never comfortable for me when I feel that things have been left unsaid and undone. I tried one more time, but Joey refused once again. I wondered, could I have made a clearer contact? Maybe if this had been a private session Joey wouldn't have felt so put on the spot, maybe I could have gotten more information. When this happens, it is not only the DP who feels left hanging, but it's me as well. Unfortunately, it's Joey who will lose. He must understand that the problems won't go away. Death doesn't end this!

For a change, I was able to find out the whole story instead of wondering what went wrong. This is what Michael shared with me after the séance was over: Joey's father had left his mother for another woman when Joey was very young. Joey's feelings of abandonment never left him and he had deep-seated scars. He never talked about his father; for Joey the man did not exist. Period. I thanked Michael for telling me and hoped someday Joey would deal with his anger toward his father and I knew that Joey's rudeness toward me was not personal. He had erased his father from his life; I came along and opened the door to his dead father, literally and metaphorically.

IT IS BECAUSE OF THE JOEYS OF THE WORLD THAT I STRESS the seriousness of not resolving all your relationships. Expressing your feelings of anger, disappointment and, the most important feeling of all, love, to people in your life. This applies in particular to family members, since the quality of your relationship with them will carry on throughout your life. It's our childhood experiences with parents and other significant family members and friends that set the pattern for all future relationships. The feelings that you hold on to, good or bad, but especially the ones that have damaged you, will affect every other relationship you have.

I believe it is for this reason that the family DPs are almost always the ones who come through first in a session. It is not until we begin to understand, forgive, and heal those early relationships that we can begin to understand and heal the scars and pain that are left. Additionally, we all need to understand and examine how deeply unresolved feelings affect our lives, our growth, our death, and those who are close to us. One other thought-and this is a "believe it or not"—we picked these relationships before we were born.

You are involved with your family in order to a karmic issue. What it is, I don't know, and you may not know in this life. You may not want to deal with the problem or issue, which is fine, but you will have to deal with what happens later, how a situation may escalate when the other person dies. All the tangled issues and emotions intensify when the other person becomes a DP. This is especially true if the feelings were not dealt with while the other person was alive.

We are left behind, not only conflicted with all that has happened but now confronted with no way to vent this feeling. The DP communication gives you new options. They didn't die! We all go on and communication is still possible.

What happens next? Well, some people are thrilled with this, some will refuse the open door. In the case of Joey, he had an opportunity for his father and himself to begin to understand a little about what the other felt. Joey blew it and he blew it for both of them. It is not only the living who need to communicate, confront, and resolve what was never said or dealt with.

Communication is essential if we want any relationship to grow and remain alive, otherwise, it becomes stagnant and static and will eventually wither. So my suggestion is, if you are having difficulty expressing yourselves to your mother, father, sibling, child, spouse, lover, don't wait; confront problematic issues while you are both here and alive.

Say to yourself, what would I feel if today, now, a loved one passed: anger, grief, guilt, an incredible sense of loss, and even frustration? Probably. But if you haven't said all you wanted to say before your loved one passes, then all of these feelings will escalate, leaving you in even worse shape. You'll remember all the things you had wanted to say. Actions never taken, emotional holes unfilled, thoughts left unspoken—all leave wounds deep inside us.

The purpose of this book is to help you to heal, by assuring you that if someone is already on the other side, you need have no fear, for there is no separation in love, not even by death. But it is also my purpose to emphasize the need to communicate while we are all here now, loving, infuriating, sharing, sparing, demanding, supporting, living.

There was another unresolved relationship at a séance that ended very different from Joey's. This group of people were very similar in age and interest. It was toward the end of the séance when I became aware of someone trying to come through; I felt attention being given to my ring finger. I was a little concerned, because I was ready to close the door on the other world when I could sense this new dead person anxious to get through. My ring finger began to pulsate rather quickly until I felt the presence of a young woman in spirit across the room, next to a young man named Keith who was in his late twenties. I had already noticed him at the beginning of the séance because he was so handsome. He had reddish blond hair with penetrating eyes. He was wearing cowboy boots, the fancy type with silver tips. I had noticed the tips on his boots while walking into the room because I almost fell over his feet, which in my altered state is not hard to do anyway.

I let him know there was a young woman present in her early twenties who knew him. As I attuned my mind with hers, she identified herself as Mary Beth. The quotes here are to the best of my memory of what Keith told me later, but I do remember well that there was a soft-spoken manner about her and I heard her voice tinged with what seemed to be a Southern drawl.

"Keith and I were childhood sweethearts," said Mary Beth and I repeated this to Keith. "Do you remember the large weeping willow tree down by my grandmother's pond where we counted water lilies? That day we promised we would love each other forever, and we carved our names on the side of your father's barn and later you got yelled at for that?"

I could feel the mood change in the séance as Mary Beth spoke through me of a time of adolescence, and falling in love for the first time.

Mary Beth said she had passed over into the *spirit world* by way of a car accident. Did the young man she knew as a boy remember her?

After what seemed like forever, I heard a deep sigh and Keith replied, "Mary Beth and I grew up together and were engaged to be married. We broke up not long after I went away to college. I broke her heart. Can you ask her to please forgive me?" I know it was no easy feat for him to say all this in front of a group of this size. "You can tell her yourself,'" I replied, "She can hear you."

The girl spoke again. "If we had married, I would have left you a widower. There is no need for you to feel guilt.

You were meant to be with, someone else." There was not a dry eye in the house.

Keith still needed to resolve another issue: he had been out of the country when he heard the news and had not attended her funeral. He heard about her death through a grapevine of old friends. Mary Beth wanted to reassure him that he could let all this go. She was fine and she wanted the same for him.

"I hear you are about to marry," she announced. "Yes, how did you know?" asked Keith, amazed. She philosophically replied, "We know everything that goes on with our loved ones. Dimensions don't separate us from the people we care about. Besides, I was on the committee to help pick her out for you."

Nobody in the room could hold back, they burst out loud with laughter. Congratulations were in order. The evening would end on a note of feeling that we could all move on with our respective paths and journeys, living and dead.

It is not only those left here who feel an urgency to communicate. So do the DPs, the *ones* in spirit. The DPs don't experience the same emotionality as the living, but it must be a little frustrating to have everyone think you are dead when you have only walked through a door to a different life. The only thing that changed is the system of communication. The dead folks need to express this to those left behind in life so that both those here and those in spirit can begin to let go, heal themselves, and move on.

Communicating with a loved one in spirit will not hasten your bereavement process. Only time can do that. However, knowing they are all right and that you will see them again cannot but help heal and comfort you.

There is nothing that can bring our loved ones back into their bodies, but death can never really take them from you. You'll join them when it's your time to go over to the other side. Meanwhile you can communicate with them, you just have to go about it in another way.

The comfort you can gain from this is a *supplement* to, not a *substitute* for, mourning. Mourning is a necessary process, one more segment of the relationships we make, and end and remake, as we work through our own karmic patterns.

I'm going to detour for a moment and talk about *karma*; you'll see the relevance. I want to talk about the beauty of karma. There is beauty in this universal spiritual law, the law of cause and effect, of our actions and their results, the law that influences and affects the most important learning in our lives and most certainly our relationships. But, not everyone sees the beauty. Some people don't believe at all. Others negate the power of karma. Some see it as a law of grim retribution while others use karma as an escape or excuse for not being responsible for their actions. What I have come to understand is that our karma, the cause of our actions, stays in our consciousness as we try continuously to put and keep our lives in balance. We get to "grade" ourselves in the afterlife, but we have to solve the problems here. All our past action, whether it be in this lifetime or another, will continue to exist in our souls' memory banks until we consciously address and deal with unresolved residue. Residue such as things done or not done to one another, things not dealt with, or atoned for.

When we are aware of our very real options we can stop building wrong-track karma. Some people feel it's important to know one's past lives to help this process. The DPs haven't delivered any opinions on this to me yet. Also, you the reader may not believe in reincarnation. It would be a lot easier for me to explain all of this if you did believe, but I will ask that you at the least acknowledge that there are patterns in our lives and we can consciously change the patterns. Those patterns create karma.

We can break the patterns and, even more comforting to know, God steps in. God steps in and changes or neutralizes our actions. That has created what is called the Law of Grace. Noted therapist Brian Weiss expresses this concept well:

> *When we understand reason, pattern, and causes, we experience what many call grace. The grace of understanding allows us to transcend the traditional idea of karma, so that we don't have to reenact the same old dramas. We absolve ourselves of the need to repeat them, the need to experience pain. We enter a higher flow where the key-note of our lifetimes can become one of harmony and joy.*

THOSE WHO HAVE STUDIED EASTERN RELIGIONS MAY BE MORE familiar with the word karma and the sense of being trapped on a karmic wheel. The version in the Bible simply states ". . . For whatsoever a man soweth, that shall he also reap." The equivalent within the scientific laws is, quite literally, cause and effect. However, spiritual laws are not quite as literal because essentially God is a God of forgiveness and in comes the Law of Grace.

Whenever we're in pain and can't understand how God could do this to us, it is not very consoling to reflect that it's not God punishing us, it's us, our own actions, our karma. We need to realize that it is also God that turns us around, forgiving an action that was done. It is God that steps in and balances out our actions.

Because of my work, the best example for me is the beautifully peaceful resolution the living can make with the dead. When we are at our wit's end or caught up in grief and have tried over and over to change the unfinished business with this person or situation, and we think we have nowhere to turn we find that we do.

In my fortieth year, my father had been in spirit for about eleven years and my husband had committed suicide that summer. At the time of my father's death, my relationship with him was one of anger and alienation. When I knew he was dying I never said good-bye. I carried all of that baggage with me for years.

My husband's suicide seemed to be the ultimate act of abandonment. Fortunately, by that time, I had been involved in sessions with Suzane for several years. Every session began with my father expressing his love, concern, and support. At a time when I could have felt absolutely abandoned and alone I took strength from the healthy relationship that Dad and I had been forging.

My husband had chosen to commit his ultimately selfish act in my presence. Standing three feet away from me, he shot himself. I can't expect anyone to know just how shattered and betrayed I felt. In the following weeks I began the process of rebuilding me.

After each session with Suzane I turned the cassette recording over to the psychotherapist in this intimate continuation of my relationship with my husband and exploration of my own pain and guilt.

In the beginning I believe [my psycho-therapist's] attitude was one of tolerance and curiosity, however, in time he grew respectful of the obvious benefit of this avenue of my recovery. Therapists are often frustrated when a client has no living party [with whom] to work out the deep and disturbing issues that have stagnated, often for a lifetime. It was not enough for me just to be able to say that I forgave my father for his human shortcomings in the past; I was growing stronger with my father's continuing love and support. Slowly, I was beginning to forgive my husband as well. Upon returning a tape to me one afternoon my therapist said, "Tell Suzane it is a pleasure working with her."

— Toni

THE BOTTOM LINE: YOU EITHER BELIEVE OR DON'T BELIEVE that with God all things are possible. If this is true, then the Law of Grace must and does exist. How it may happen for you, I don't know. I also don't believe it is important to know how. I do believe your actions will not go unnoticed and that the Law of Grace does and will exist because of the love God holds for us. If prolonged entrapment on the wheel of karma, endless repetitions of life scenarios were truly the case, I believe we would never have the chance to grow because we would be constantly trying to undo everything we had done.

I'm not saying you are not responsible for your actions. You are, period. I am saying that if you have given everything to honestly confront the action and deal with a situation, then you won't carry this with you when you go into spirit or another lifetime.

There are those who don't believe karma is changeable, and that they must accept their fate, their circumstances. This is not true: karma is changeable, forgiveness does heal and change the karma, and thus we have Grace.

Once again we come back to our own relationships with God, our sense of what our souls are. What a great gift God has given us! Remember it and you will stay in balance with what is true for you on your individual path and journey:

▲ You are responsible for your own actions.

▲ Your actions affect yourself and others.

▲ You can change.

▲ You can be forgiven.

▲ You can forgive yourself.

Forgiveness: the never-ending message.

IT WAS TIME FOR MY FOUR O'CLOCK APPOINTMENT. THE doorbell rang and there stood a young woman. She was small, simply dressed and had an accent that I guessed to be Hispanic. She sat down and I explained what I do and prepared for opening my wires. I immediately felt the presence of and then the smell of smoke, not the smell I pick up with cigarette smoke but the smell of burning wood. I heard through my inner ear the word *fire* followed by *brother*.

Within moments I felt this man's presence. He had an exceptionally strong physique and the air of one who took impeccable care of his physical appearance. He also seemed very aware of this, for he commented several times on his looks, humorously but proudly. He had died in a fire, he said, but this was not an ordinary fire. Many had passed with him but he only knew one of them. This all confused me, but I hoped that as he went on the pieces would fall into place. The other message he wanted to express was that he had known somehow what was going to happen to him.

I then received the feeling that this was his sister sitting across from me. The other message he needed to pass on was how much he loved her and how much he wanted her forgiveness. Forgiveness for what wasn't clear at this point. He hoped she understood his weakness. Since I sensed him as being so strong it was hard to imagine him being weak, but I was only passing along the message. It was not my job to figure it all out.

His sister said she wanted his forgiveness. She was sorry she had been so judgmental toward him. Did he know that she nonetheless loved him deeply? He then wanted to ask about his sons and wife. She said they were fine but missed him deeply. Again, in some connection to his wife and children, he wanted his sister's forgiveness.

At this point I asked her if she understood what he was telling me. She assured me she did.

He spoke of having had a vision. He thought it was

Jesus. He had known at the time it meant he would have to change his ways. He wanted Jesus to forgive him. He was sorry he hurt her, as well as his family, but he couldn't let the other woman go. He loved his family but still he loved this other woman who boosted his ego tremendously. He spoke poetically of their homeland, then added that their father was there in spirit with him and he too was fine. The stronger messages continued. "I died from the smoke, not the flames. Did you get the roses I sent?"

His sister was no longer able to hold back the tears. "Yes, and I'm so sorry, Phillipe. They were beautiful. How is our father?"

"He is here with me and we are fine."

She was begging for his forgiveness even while he said it was he who needed hers. Would she watch over his sons? "My wife is a good woman, I just loved another. Please tell my sons I love them."

At the end of the session she told me the story. She knew her brother had had a vision before his death. Three days before, he had sent her roses and said he was coming home. She explained that when he got involved with the other woman he had not been welcome in her home. She had gotten the roses with a note asking for her forgiveness and promising that he was going to leave the woman and try to patch things up with his wife and family. She had been so happy then. This situation had put so much stress on the family she couldn't wait to see him. That night he died in one of the biggest mass fires in New York City. She never got to see him again.

I couldn't possibly begin to count the lives and experiences that have been changed after séances, whether in private or in a group. In session after session, as the DPs come through, I hear the living say, "If only." However, the only "if onlys" we have control over are expressing our feelings to those we love and resolving issues that need resolving, so that when death occurs, however it occurs, we are complete. I mean that in terms of our own deaths, the deaths of those we love, and the deaths of those with whom peace was never possible. There are many paths to resolution; it isn't important how completely we succeed, it is important, how completely we try.

Following one séance, I received a phone call from a young woman who had been deeply touched when the DPs she loved showed up. The only family she had-the ones who adopted her-had all passed over within a year's time-her mother, father, and brother. Their deaths had devastated her. She had just given birth to her first child and wished that they could have shared in her new extended family. She knew nothing about her birth family and had no desire to know either. She never wanted to seek out and find them. She had known for most of her life that she had been adopted, but, to her, she already had the best family she could find.

During the séance her family came through and told her quite clearly that if she were ready, her birth family, still living, wanted to contact her. Naturally, during the séance this was a bit confusing for me, because it was her adopted family who was giving me the information and I didn't know she was adopted. However, she seemed to know exactly what they meant and explained it to me later. Her main problem was her conflict about whether to go through with the contact.

In the end, she had trusted those in spirit and agreed to make a call that could possibly open up the doors for her to reconnect with her birth family. Within a month's time, she met her birth mother and discovered she also had a brother. This brought up many issues and unresolved feelings, but she was also being presented with everything she felt she had lost a family. It would not be the same, but it would help. She and her birth mother (at this point there was no contact with the father) worked to put into balance all the feelings that went with the giving up of a child. The sense of family, the togetherness she so missed was now coming back. She called me again shortly after this meeting to let me know what had resulted from the séance. God does work in mysterious ways! My last story, Marilyn's story, is another example.

Marilyn, at the age of 42, was dying of cancer after five years of hope, chemotherapy, and disappointment. As a young woman, she had left her family out West to try her wings in New York. Shy and quiet at first, she had over the years blossomed into a highly successful public relations executive. Her family, however, had early on written her out of their lives. She had left behind her stem religion and she had for a while lived with a man outside of marriage though later she had married someone else. Her sister had informed her that she would burn in hell. All that Marilyn had was a tenuous contact with her mother and brother.

And now she was dying. Her father did not return her phone calls. Her mother, who had in recent years become emotionally dependent on Marilyn, was completely unable to deal with the reality of the cancer. Her sister wouldn't talk to her. No one would come to visit her in New York, so a few months before her death Marilyn made the effort to fly back home to try to resolve the wounds within her family. She felt she made a little progress, but only a little.

Close to the end, a group of friends decided to have a special ceremony for Marilyn and with Marilyn, a prayer circle in her home. Eight people gathered: one flew in from California, another delayed a trip to Paris, another cancelled a business trip; all would give their wholehearted attention and time to Marilyn.

As the friends planned for Marilyn's evening, I was asked to be there. Marilyn had taken part in séances where her much-loved grandmother, who had died when Marilyn was a young teenager, came through. As much as Marilyn had tried to deal with her family's problems, she also knew that death meant she was going home to join her grandmother.

Her husband Robert met us at the door. He told us to expect the worst since she was incoherent and would probably not know what was going on. We put Native American music on the stereo because Marilyn's childhood home was in desert country and she loved the serene rhythms of flute and drum.

In her bedroom, we found a Marilyn who was not incoherent, but awake, attentive, and full of happiness. She was in pain as well but focused on her joy that we were there. We asked her to close her eyes, and, as she lay there, her friends told her of their love for her and the meaning she held in their lives. They told her they were gathered to give her love, to let her go, and to offer their prayers and support in her journey into the light. As Marilyn lay there, listening, her grandmother came through in spirit. "Marilyn," I told her, "your grandmother is standing beside you." As Marilyn's eyes lit up, I said, "Marilyn, she's telling you, don't be afraid, she will be there waiting for you." We had to stop soon after. Marilyn was tiring fast.

We went into the next room, and Marilyn's friends continued to read poems and talk about her importance to them. We are her family, they told Robin, Marilyn belonged to all of them. Robin broke down. We all sat in a circle, silent, holding hands, and praying.

As the ceremony was ending, one of the friends told me what Marilyn had written to him a year and a half earlier: she had had a dream, and in that dream her grandmother had come to her and told Marilyn she would be there to help her all along the way.

Marilyn had wanted so badly to have her family be there, to find healing and love together. That didn't happen. They wouldn't come. But in the end, I believe Marilyn got her wish-a circle of friends who gathered to do her honor and to help her as lovingly as they knew how. She will carry that love with her as her grandmother waits. (By the time this book went to press, Marilyn passed over.)

Marilyn's story, and all the others, illustrate what to me is a fundamental truth: that séances are as much about life as about death. Facing our own deaths, enduring another's, we must learn to trust that all this is in greater hands and let go. Hopefully, the knowledge that our loved ones can communicate with us now and that they will wait for us when the time comes for our own journeys into the light will ease our own fears of death and ease the pain of losing those we love. The knowledge that "death" is not the end will hopefully influence the way we choose to live our lives.

I know all too well how difficult this is for most people to believe, accept, or understand. I also know that these are the simple truths I've learned from the DPs. By listening to yourself, you'll know what is right for you and for those you love. The most important relationship you have is with yourself, and you do have control to change and grow. You can't control others. Change in a relationship requires both people to want to deal with issues that are painful and difficult. If only one of the parties is willing to do this, and you are that one, you will have to search in your heart and know you've done all you can do.

Life is a funny thing. There are people who want nothing to do with their families and then there are others who will try everything to get a mother or a father to love them. There are those who simply refuse to attempt to heal a relationship that has left them angry their whole lives. And then there are others who would do anything for the chance to mend fences and to share once again with those loved ones.

All too often it takes the death of someone you love to make you realize the importance of sharing our feelings. It's not easy to accept this and it's not easy to begin the process of trying to put these feelings into balance. It's even harder to consider the possibility of communicating with those loved ones in the *spirit world*.

Still, the DPs and I want you to know it's *never* too late to say, "I love you" or "Forgive me."

Walk your path, and follow the road that takes a different turn for each of us, and, please, please remember, love cannot be separated by death. I have that on the best of information.

Chapter 14

Responsibility

The DPs

IN THE BEGINNING OF MY CAREER AS A trance-medium, the DPs made some mention of responsibility, but it wasn't the focal point it seems to have become for them now. In those early days, it seemed only an occasional concern.

Many constant themes come through in the voices of those in the Afterlife (i.e., love, reassurance, comfort, and a sense of closure). Within the last few years, though, something else has been building. Not added, *building*—coming through stronger. As though there is a momentum in the redefining of love. And in addition, adding a momentum in the determination of those who have died.

The DPs are not philosophizing about larger existential meanings. They lived their own lives day by month by year, experiencing joy and sorrow in piercing moments or the unremarkable episodes which, accumulated, become a life. Some are the George's of *It's a Wonderful Life*, heroic in small ways. Some are suicides, offering consolation that they are not eternally damned. Some are hated parents, relatives once unyielding and judgmental. Some are great-grandparents and siblings we might never have known we had. Some were lonely, some were loved beyond all measure. They belonged to us, and because, as "forever" weaves through "now," we still belong to them, they want to help us in our lives.

The DPs are adding new urgency, new meaning to the message of love. They realize their mistakes and they want to help the living. That is part of the Afterlife process, the life review. It is apparently humbling, and for some painful. Some of the DPs turn away from reassessing their lives, and as they turn, look back to the living left behind. How clear it is to them the mistakes the living are making. They, the DPs did much the same. Now, they want to help the living, but they cannot interfere with the life process of those still on earth. Everyone has their own path. The DPs know and respect this, but it's frustrating. They can indicate truth but can't force acceptance.

The DPs realize all the patterns and the mutual responsibilities once they cross over. The living have a much harder time with the concept. Many of the living are out there buying books on the subject. Listening to their DPs is probably not an option they know they have.

There is a *cosmic window* open now. A framework has been built by recent events and certain traditions that have readied us for what those who have lived and left their lives have to tell. It was not always so and the window will close again. We have a great need *and* responsibility to hear the messages now and, in the DPs estimation, we are more able than ever before to hear it, to truly absorb and understand it. If—and it's a big *if*—we want to.

The DPs have always been able to reassure us about their welfare. They won't be continuing this process forever. Two reasons: It's not their job—they have their paths, we have ours. Secondly, it won't always work. Timing, in the sense of our readiness to hear, is a crucial factor.

Heading into this millennium, we are working our way out of the excesses of prior decades dedicated to extreme selfishness. People faced with too little time in the day have zeroed in on quality time. The one with the most meaningful experiences, not toys, wins. That was the product of the mid-'90s. By the late '90s, another fad had surfaced, the theme of responsibility as a life-enhancing virtue.

In the search for new direction, old ways and old answers are not enough anymore. The return to religion is much cited, yet many religions, and many moral statements, are based less on love than on inequality: there are the blessed, the chosen, the righteous, those with promised clouds in the right neighborhoods of heaven—and then there's the rest of us. "Spirituality," which enfolds religion and so many other ways to peace, is a richer term for both the searching and the answer.

The window of opportunity will close eventually because humanity, restless in intellect and interests, will move on to other things. It seems to be the way we do things, in steps forward and steps back. The more we can learn and retain now, while this "fad" of spiritual hunger and yearning for fulfilled lives endures, the more we can build our true inner selves and a foundation of integrity for the future.

With these things in mind, I have interwoven six messages throughout this book to help get across what the DPs want us to know. They are:

- ▲ The role of the DPs—what they can and can't do for us.

- ▲ There is a right place and a right time for everything.

- ▲ What happens in life happens, in part, because we chose it to happen.

- ▲ Who are we? What do the DPs see when they look back?

- ▲ The DPs ask the living to come to terms with taking responsibility for life.

- ▲ Don't be afraid.

The DPs see people surrounded by possessions. Busy families who forget to leave room in the schedule for joy, who delay togetherness until tomorrow. Happiness is sought in many guises but sharing of love is temporarily delayed due to many things, depending on the individual. Then one of two things happens. Positively, we turn to spiritual values to nourish the drought in our own value system. And negatively, the other road is to say, "Well, it's not my fault," and think who or what we can blame.

The major lesson to learn from dealing with death is to reiterate the responsibility you have to show care and compassion in life. The nature of the insights depends on the nature of those who are giving advice and telling their side of the stories. Their side is the *other side.*

Take responsibility, the DPs say. It's your life, and you are meant to live it with love, giving love. It comes down to value yourself, value others—and live in a way that reflects both.

Oprah Winfrey once commented wryly that all her pains and difficulties stemmed from her not valuing herself. What I know now is that every bit of pain I have experienced in my life was a result of me worrying about what another person was going to think of me. For others, the fear can be of commitment; of being asked to be or do or give what we cannot, or choose not to offer of ourselves.

Any help we can get with that one, we ought to take.

The Medium

Taking control of your life—being responsible for your own life—is one of the primary mantras of self-esteem and self-help books. This book's difference lies in the *source* of the advice. I have intended for it to be an aid to your life *here.* The wise words come through me as the conduit, putting those in the *Spirit World* on speakerphone for you, the living. How can I write this? Because, I am a trance medium with a conscience.

It's not in me to do anything halfway. I can't just sit in a room with someone and simply say "There is someone standing behind you that loves you, and is stroking your hair, smiling." You would think I was full of *crap*. I feel I have been given this gift with an added responsibility to give those I "sit" with the most specific information and messages I can.

I personally believe that mediums must have some unwritten or untold code they follow in delivering messages from the *Afterlife* and DPs. I also feel very strongly that we must give great attention to the way we pass on the information we receive. That it is done in a most responsible way. We also have the responsibility of taking the best care of ourselves in order to do what we do at its highest level, and to *stand tall* in and around our integrity of what we do.

I believe we are not to give out messages about impending or perceived death. I remember one such psychic medium appearing on a television show, and when asked if she knew anything about the disappearance of someone's daughter, telling the parent that she was dead. Of course, they were devastated. The problem, and irresponsibility of this, was that the daughter was found not to be dead two weeks later. Think of what this family went through for two weeks!

Although it has been good in many ways that the media has brought mediumship to the foreground, there is some room for learning about their part of the responsibility. Mediums have been held in the highest *place* throughout time. During Houdini's prominence, there were thousands visible everywhere. Their information was valued. It is only now because of the universal technology we have, that mediumship is much more *in our face*.

There was a degree of separation until the recent events of September 11 in the U.S. For most of us, experiencing death and later grief, was kept in a more personal realm. With the horror of watching what happened on that day, *as it was happening*, here in our own home, the *Great Mystery* called death was brought to the forefront of our existence. Grief and mourning were escalated. Where we had previously processed our grief on a more individual, personal level, we now have been thrown into dealing with or *not* dealing with it *en masse*.

This tragedy combined with the *open window* I talked about earlier, sets about a sense of higher responsibility, I feel, we mediums have in relation to the living. We can provide an avenue of closure for those who have no physical bodies to do so. Cemeteries are for the living, and oftentimes those who have no physical body to relate to remain in excruciating pain and sorrow needlessly for years. Some a lifetime.

Many think because mediums, like myself, are in contact with those who have *crossed over* that we are eliminated from our own mournings. No way! We just know without a doubt that we don't die—cease to exist. We also have to process that lack of physical presence just as anyone else. Grief comes down to an individual process and there are no quick rules for it. A loss is a loss. We all need to honor that process. And, I believe through determination, time and trust, doors of connection can be available to all of us. God gives us free will. We create our belief systems. We can choose to stay in or not in a certain framework. When things hit us personally, it is dealt with in a very, very different framework. We can honor our grief process or we can be in denial.

Grief is *knowing* you loved someone. Some take unhealed grief and redirect or divert themselves to addictive behaviors and activities. We ultimately decide if we want to hear those messages or not. Our responsibility is to do the best we possibly can to come to terms and deal with death and loss; knowing that there are some deaths we will never ultimately get over. They will leave a big hole in our hearts, but that is our responsibility to heal.

Here is a final example of resistance to hearing the message and choosing denial:

> One woman came to me who was so upset over her son's death that she'd transferred her grief into compulsive gambling. She refused to process. Every weekend, she was on the bus to Atlantic City. She was by now in major debt, and also in denial she had a problem. This didn't help her relationship with her husband either. I think, from what her son in spirit told me, that it was only he who kept them together. They both had loved him but had long since forgotten about loving each other. When he died, they began to drift apart. In this case, silence was not golden.

> During our session, the boy tried to talk to his mother about the gambling, but she kept changing the subject. He was persistent, but she was more so. She only wanted to hear repeated over and over that he was safe and well now, and how she wanted him to know how much she missed him. She did not want to hear that he had thoughts on where her missing him was leading, or that he would ever give advice to his mother on her life style. She didn't come back for another session. This

new relationship between her son and herself was not one she wanted. I don't know what happened to her. With most clients, I don't; they go their own ways. But, I got the sense that for her it wouldn't be anything good.

THE DPs BRING THEIR MESSAGES. BOTTOM LINE IS WE HEAR what we want to hear. It really comes to the point that we can give somebody a message and they are going to read into it how they want it to read. If they are not ready or willing to hear it, then they will just continue *being* where they are. If someone is shutdown or afraid, it can have a major affect on receiving information that could enable them to heal and move on. Someone who does the work I do can only offer you an opportunity to continue to have a relationship. The communication just happens to be on a different level.

Epilogue

THERE IS A PROCESS OF EVOLVEMENT within our consciousness about physical death going on. The *window* of opportunity at this moment is open for deeper understanding. Since death has been the greatest mystery of all, I do believe that we are now in a period of time in terms of consciousness, tied in with technology and the world, that offers the vastness of that mystery to become smaller. In the world of today, the great mystery is definitely more confrontive and *in our face*. Obviously, current events have had such an impact on a mass level, that we can no longer keep death totally personal and at arm's length.

I have been shown over and over again to what extent the DPs will go in an effort to let the living know they are *just fine*, and to get their other messages across. So, in essence, this book *is* a guide for the living. After all, it's how death affects us all, whether from mass passings like the World Trade Towers in New York, or to our more personal ones. The DPs will use any possible way from dreams, to visitations, songs played, smells, electrical outbursts, or the neighbor's children to let us know they are in fact "all right." Our job, the more difficult and often more painful one, is to *listen* to the other messages sometimes offered. That's a huge responsibility.

Just dealing with our own personal grief, and personally trusting/knowing without a doubt that we have in some way been contacted can open the door to a *second* chance of communication and connection. If that contact comes from a medium, and the medium is authentic, just know that the DPs are working very hard to let the living know they are there.

Of course, the medium has the large responsibility of being "together" enough to be the best *receiver* possible. This is not a "wing it" job. After all, you have precious souls with you that are anxious to receive a message. I believe if the person receiving the message suddenly goes *brain dead*, you give them the message anyway. They'll most likely figure it out later.

Which brings me to a point. If you are in a session, group, or lecture where a medium is delivering a message and you feel the message is for you, although someone else has raised their hand, then the message is most likely *for* you.

I remember doing a lecture in South Florida and toward the end was doing some questions and answer time. I had

worked my way to the back of the room where a gentle-
man was sitting. The information I was picking up was
something about a son, about a father and a "passing." It
seemed to be the father of the man before me was sharing
about a son and a car accident. The man became so upset
that he quite literally broke down, even to the point where
I couldn't really understand what he was saying. It was
pretty intense. It affected a lot of people in the room, and
we never got to finish.

Two days later, the woman who was in charge of my
seminars received a call from the man in Florida. He left
his number, and asked if I would call him back. I did, and
his first words were "You saved my life and gave me a
second chance." He then proceeded to tell me what happened. He had a son who was a navy pilot, and lived with
him after a bitter divorce. One day they'd had a big fight
and in the midst of it, the father told the son to get the hell
out, and not come back. The young man, who I think was
called Danny, was about 22. He took off and the father
hadn't made contact for many years; six or seven.

It seems after the seminar, the father was moved to
call his ex-wife thinking what he had heard from me
might have to do with his son. He had had no contact
with her in years also. He went straight to the point. Did
she have any information regarding their son's whereabouts? She proceeded to tell the father that after the son
had come to her, he had had a major car accident that had
left him mentally around the age of 17. Since that time, he
had gone through rehabilitation and was now living in
Georgia on his own, and working at a Wendy's fast food
restaurant.

This news was devastating to the father and he immediately felt immense guilt about their last time together and his absence of the past years. He managed to get the information of where in Georgia his son was and the exact address of the Wendy's. After a 15-hour drive that had lasted through the night, he found the one. It just happened his son was working the 7 A.M. shift. (There are no coincidences.) He stood for a moment watching, barely holding back the tears before he went over, and hugged Danny. He told him how sorry he was, and that he was there to help him in anyway he could.

His words to me were "My God, my son needs me, and I feel I am being given a second chance to be there for him." He thanked me for the "message."

The DPs tell me we are in an era when a greater number of people than ever before are open to spirituality and an idealism in which "enrichment" is more apt to describe a fulfilled life than a financially successful life. They look at how we have been busy with getting and winning, self-promoting and self-involved, refusing commitment, denying responsibility, throwing off blame like uncomfortable shoes because truth often pinches. They see families falling apart and failing, fighting over money, older and younger generations with nothing in common except resentment. They watch their children and children's children get married and have more children. Then they watch relative A cutting off relative B from family interaction, not for any cogent reason, but to punish them. Who loses out? We all do.

I love what I do and I love how I can help others in their loss processes. I love seeing relationships healed and reconnected. I truly believe that in this work, if one has lost the passion and patience to deal with those fragile folks that come to you, then one should consider doing something else. Yes, I may get flack. Those times when there is ridicule, disbelief, and fingers pointing saying you are crazy—all that accompanies this profession—but I know I could never find one I feel more privileged and honored to do. To connect someone with a loved one who is no longer in their physical body is without question, just that.

Take responsibility, the DPs are saying. Take control of your own life. They are here to say you are meant to live it with love, giving love. It comes down to value yourself, value others, and live in a way that reflects both.

It is my responsibility to bring the DPs' messages. It is the responsibility of the living to listen to those messages. Sometimes, the message is abrupt. Sometimes it goes on for several sessions. The stories I hear reveal all the nooks and crannies in personal pride, pain, and self-determination. There is a core challenge in the idea of self-help, it seems to me. The "help" means change; we have to want to take the risk of changing ourselves; the repair and healing of our relationships. Not everyone is.

For those who do listen to the DPs, the rewards range from peace of mind to life-affirming joy. We all truly *do* have the opportunity for a *second chance*. It quite simply is our choice whether we take it or not.

About the Author

Suzane Northrop is a nationally recognized trance medium, an expert in psychic phenomena, and has worked as a consultant for numerous police departments throughout the country. For the past 25 years, she has worked deligently in her effort to help bridge the gap between the world of the living and the spirit world. She has lectured extensively in the United States and Great Britain, to groups including New York University's Anthropological Society, New York Women's Bar Association, the Spiritual Frontier Fellowship, and both the American and British Societies for Physical Research. She has also been a favorite guest on numerous television programs, including *Extra, Entertainment Tonight, The Leeza Show, National Enquirer TV,* Fox Family Channel, MSNBC, The Discovery Channel, and an HBO documentary, entitled *Life After Life.* In addition, she has hosted a pilot for cable television, and acted as consultant for Demi Moore for *The Butcher's Wife.* Suzane currently makes her home in New York City.

To learn more about Suzane Northrop, visit her Website
www.suzanenorthrop.com